The Handbook for
FLOWER ARRANGERS

The Handbook for
FLOWER ARRANGERS

[with 123 photographs in colour]

Compiled by
PHYLLIS PAGE

BLANDFORD PRESS
POOLE   DORSET

Blandford Press Ltd,
Link House, West Street,
Poole, Dorset BH15 1LL

First published 1965
Second (revised) Edition 1971
Reprinted 1974
Third (revised) Edition 1976

Dedicated to
ELSIE PHIPPS
whose inspiration and encouragement
set me off on the road of colour
photography of flower arrangements

Text set in 11pt Baskerville,
printed and bound by
Richard Clay (The Chaucer Press), Ltd
Bungay, Suffolk.

ISBN 0 7137 07658

CONTENTS

CONTENTS

PREFACE

The interest in flower arrangement gains momentum every year and over the years has changed from a local drawing-room activity to a nationwide and international art. In Great Britain this is due mainly to the formation of the National Association of Flower Arrangement Societies of Great Britain, whose help and inspiration I acknowledge.

A flower arrangement is a thing of passing beauty which rarely lasts longer than a few days; in this book I have tried to capture forever some outstanding arrangements.

It is, of course, only possible to include a selection of the wonderful arrangements that have graced the shows, cathedrals, churches and famous houses up and down the country. It is not always a first prize entry that makes the best photograph or picture, so arrangements by novices as well as expert arrangers have been included, giving a variety which I hope will have an appeal to all flower lovers.

Some of the arrangements have been photographed at shows where the lighting and background were not ideally suitable for reproduction but as some of these are particularly beautiful I felt it would be a pity not to include them.

I have invited well-known flower arrangers to contribute chapters on various aspects and types of flower arrangement, and I am indebted to them for their co-operation. These are arranged broadly according to season. As one chapter may relate to another, it is not possible to place all the pictures in text order but references are given at the end of each chapter to the appropriate illustrations.

7

Description of the arrangements illustrated follow the colour section. I would like to thank the flower arrangers who have so willingly given me permission to reproduce their work and have supplied details of the flowers and plants used.

My friends overseas, whose letters and exchanges of photographs have brought many fresh ideas, have written most informative and stimulating chapters on flower arranging in their countries with photographs to illustrate them.

Acknowledgments are due to the following:

His Grace the Duke of Marlborough for permission to reproduce photographs taken in Blenheim Palace.

The Vicar of the Parish of St John the Baptist, Cirencester, for permission to reproduce photographs taken during the Festival of Flowers.

Mr Ian MacCallum, Director of the American Museum in Britain, Claverton Manor, Bath, for permission to reproduce photographs taken in the Museum during the National Festival, 'Flowers and Costume'.

The Geffrye Museum for permission to reproduce the photograph taken in one of the period rooms.

In this latest edition I am fortunate to have the opportunity to add a chapter on abstract design, with some new photographs, thus bringing the book up to date.

I am grateful to Mrs Brunskill and Mrs Gough for their help. I would also like to thank my publishers for their help and enthusiasm, and in particular Miss Vera Frampton for her gentle guidance.

Phyllis C Page

I . SPRING

SPRING FLOWERS

George W. Smith

The most welcome flowers of all are those of spring as they appear at a time of year when we crave for colour and fragrance after the drabness of winter. They have unfortunately earned the reputation of being short-lived and difficult to arrange. This is probably because nature has equipped many of them with strong straight stems and spear-like leaves specially adapted to pierce hard soil; also, since many bloom out of doors in cool conditions, the texture of their petals is ill-suited to heated rooms.

Let us consider their advantages. Many spring flowers are bulbous subjects forming part of a botanical group of plants called monocotyledons, a marked characteristic of this group being that their cells are arranged in parallel veins. This cell structure enables them to drink water more easily than plants with more complex cell systems, thus they are well suited to being arranged on pinholders and in shallow containers. Their clear shape and often strong colour give them a distinct personality, while their perfume, developed to attract pollinating insects which are scarce at this time, is also greatly appreciated by flower-lovers.

The importance of conditioning plant material is often overlooked. All cut flowers need several hours in deep water in a cool place before arranging. It is advisable to remove all the white portion from the stem tips of bulbous subjects. Iris and tulips are particularly inclined to wilt if

9

this is not done. For woody-stemmed material, such as forced lilac and guelder rose (*Viburnum opulus*), it is essential to split the stem tip by using a knife or hammer and then place the blossom stems in two inches of very hot water. Choose a deep pail for this process, filling it up with cold water after ten minutes. Protect the actual blooms from steam with tissue paper. This is also a most effective way of reviving wilted woody-stemmed material – generally, the stronger the stem the warmer the water to be used. Warm water may also be used to revive soft-stemmed flowers and will produce results where cold water fails, anemones being a case in point.

Tulips are particularly difficult to condition and it should be borne in mind that they grow in water when cut, thus altering their position. This can be very graceful for traditional arrangement but useless when a stylized effect is desired.

Early forced branches of blossom of flowering currant, horse chestnut, and various species of prunus and forsythia, to name but a few, can be most attractive, and cost little in time or expense. Immerse the entire branch in warm water overnight in the bath. This process will soften the gummy solution protecting the bud and enable the embryo leaves or blossom to develop. Catkins have a pendant elegance of their own and will develop in water without immersion; the hedgerow hazel or the green tassels of *Garrya elliptica* are most attractive.

Foliage is essential to almost all spring flower arrangements, providing a foil to their beauty. Very young leaves are never easy to condition, therefore try to select the more mature growth. Forced leaves of various species of hosta are interesting, while wild arums, *Begonia rex* and aspidistra are familiar to every flower arranger. The humble bergenias (winter saxifrages) provide outdoor foliage often tinted to a liverish hue by cold conditions. These, coupled with evergreen leaves of *Iris foetidissima variegata*, *Arum pictum* and *A. italicum*, *Ruta graveolens* 'Jackman's Blue' and many varieties of ivy, too numerous to mention, are all essential plants to the flower arranger seeking early leaves. The florist can also provide a wealth of foliage to enhance our flowers including camellia, ruscus, grevillea, pittosporum and many species of eucalyptus.

Some brief mention must be made of the beauty of early shrubs. The Japanese witch hazel (*Hamamelis molis*) with its yellow spider-like flowers is the first to flower and is followed by the mauve *Daphne mezereum* and the fragrant white species. The graceful arching stems of winter jasmine last well in water. The attractive coloured barks of dog-wood (*Cornus sanguinea*), several willows and broom all add interest.

So much for what to grow and how to condition. The type and style of arrangement will be governed by the purpose for which it is intended and the setting it is to fill. This may be greatly varied, from the simple to the opulent. The choice of container will depend on the material that is available for the arrangement. Startling effects can be achieved with modern glass of exciting colour, designed mainly for the contemporary setting. There is a simple rusticity in woven baskets and hand-made pottery which makes them a natural choice for the cottage home; old metal containers of pewter, copper and brass, together with wooden bowls and boxes, are also appropriate. For those with scope to decorate on a sophisticated or lavish scale urns, tazzas, comportes and ewers of metal, marble and porcelain are ideal. The delicacy of Dresden and Minton figures is well suited to support fragrant and subtle mixtures of spring treasures, echoing their form or colouring. It is often the addition of an unusual leaf or flower that adds a note of distinction to any arrangement. For instance, green and mauve hellebores and *Lysichitum* look striking with a sculptured arum flower in yellow or white.

Iris stylosa and *I. reticulata*, miniature cyclamen and fritillaries are easily grown out of doors, but there are also greenhouse bulbs possessing wonderful colour that are not difficult to grow, such as shell-pink veltheimia or the lime-green and russet *Lachenalia pearsonii*, to name only two.

The diversity of plant material and numerous styles of arrangement may seem baffling to the beginner but charming, often quite simple, effects can be achieved with a little knowledge and much patience. Always strive to create beauty by emulating nature and natural growth, which provide a constant source of inspiration.

The following photographs are examples:
2, 3, 23, 39, 57, 62

SIMPLE ARRANGEMENTS

Beryl Jackman

The first requirements for an arrangement are plant material, a container and something to hold the flowers and foliage in position. Most arrangements are made up of three types of plant material: fine, pointed material for the outline, filling-in material and important flowers or foliage to make a centre of interest.

For the outline, use foliage such as privet, ivy or iris leaves and branches of forsythia or pussy willow. Bare branches and grasses will serve the same purpose. The function of this outline material is to lead your eye to the centre of interest. The filling-in material may be medium-sized flowers such as freesias, sprays of mimosa or clusters of berries or interesting foliage. For the centre of interest, large, round flowers should be used, for example tulips or chrysanthemums; large leaves may serve either as the focal point or to back up the central flowers and give visual weight to the base of the arrangement.

The next consideration is the container and pinholder or wire. When the container is shallow a pinholder should be fixed by placing four small knobs of Plasticine on the bottom of the pinholder, which is then pressed down hard on to the container with a screwing motion. The pinholder and container must be absolutely clean and dry or the Plasticine will not stick. Crumpled two-inch mesh chicken wire should be settled firmly into a deeper container. A pinholder at the bottom is desirable though not essential.

Now for your arrangement. First decide on your design. There are various conventional ones in flower arrangement made up of straight lines or curves. Vertical, horizontal and triangular arrangements are in the former group; crescent and Hogarth curve in the latter. In making an arrangement of any design, all the material should flow from one point, in front of which should be the centre of interest, usually low down and beneath the tallest placement.

A vertical design is perhaps the simplest of all. Use a container which is shallow and wide, putting a pinholder in the centre. If you are using a dish which does not hold enough water, the pinholder can be placed in a small bowl or a painted tin. First make the outline. Three pieces of pussy willow of varying lengths are suitable. Place the tallest in the centre, about two-thirds of the way back on the pinholder. The height should be about one and a half times the *width* of the container, not less, but if it is fine material it may be more. The other two pieces should be placed one on each side of and close to the first. Five or six irises or tulips may now be placed in front of the leaves, graduated in height and not immediately one below the other but slightly 'staggered'. A bud should be at the top and the largest flower low at the base to form the centre of interest. If tulips are used, the petals of the lowest ones may be turned back carefully to add importance. Large leaves such as bergenia, laurel or arum are needed to give more weight to the base; remember to put one or two at the back of the pinholder to give depth to the arrangement. Some filling-in material can be recessed round the lower flowers. This design can also be made in a tall narrow container, but this is more difficult for a beginner.

A simple triangular arrangement requires three pieces

of fine foliage, one for the centre upright and the other two pieces for the 'arms', about two-thirds the length of the main branch. These should be placed horizontally at each side but coming slightly forward in order to give depth to the arrangement. To place them at an angle on the pinholder cut the stems at a slant, put them upright on the pins and press them down to the desired position. Imagine a triangle within the three points of the outline and all other material should be within this to keep the design. Working towards the centre, still with all the stems flowing out from one point, fill in with medium flowers and foliage, finishing low at the centre with the largest flowers and foliage which should be directly beneath the tallest placement. Do not forget to make some flowers and foliage flow forward and recess others to give the arrangement a third dimension. This design can also be used in a pedestal-type container, where the height of the container governs the length of the main branch. This should be one and a half times the height of the container, plus enough stem to go down into the water. Always remember to allow some flowers and foliage to flow over the rim of the container.

An asymmetrical triangle is made in the same way but one side piece should be shorter than the other with heavier leaves placed on the shorter side to balance the longer side. If a shallow container is used then place the pinholder to one side to achieve balance.

A horizontal arrangement may be made in a bread-tin or similar, fairly low, container, filled with chicken wire. The side pieces should be long, flowing forward and down, but the upright should be very short; fill in towards the centre of interest which is low down. A horizontal arrangement may also be made in a candle-cup on a candle-stick, with the flowers and foliage flowing down over the rim of the candle-cup. The total width of this arrangement should be one and a half times the height of the candle-stick.

The crescent speaks for itself. When using a shallow container the outline is made from two curved pieces of foliage. Broom is ideal for this. One piece should be longer than the other, the tip of the longer one coming over the centre of the pinholder and the shorter one continuing the crescent on the opposite side. It is advisable to use only a few flowers, following the line of the crescent, with buds at the outer ends of the curve and full-blown flowers as the centre of interest, which should be below the tip of the longer arm. Smaller flowers or foliage can be used to back up the central flowers and hide the pinholder but they must always follow the curve.

A Hogarth curve, which is known as the 'Lazy S', is made on a tall container such as a candle-stick or tall goblet. It is similar to a crescent but the outline is turned downwards and forwards to form a rough S-shape. The focal point is beneath the tip of the top placement which should come above the centre of the container. Again the flowers should follow the curves of the outline with the largest blooms in the centre. It is advisable to use wire and a pinholder for this design.

All flower arrangements are based on the fundamental shapes described, however simple or complicated they may be. It is not necessary to use an abundance of flowers in order to achieve an artistic effect; this is an advantage in the winter months when flowers are scarce.

The following photographs are examples:
2, 4, 5, 6, 7, 36, 37, 50

INTERPRETATIVE DESIGNS

Iona Trevor Jones

A popular section of most flower arrangement exhibitions is that devoted to interpretative designs. It calls for great originality and ingenuity; the scope of portraying quotations, song titles, precious jewels, etc., is limitless.

Never confuse well-staged gimmicks with genuine originality, and remember the flowers are more important than the accessories.

To sacrifice such principles as good design and colour blending at the expense of pure drama and impact is one of the most common faults, but do not go to the opposite extreme and concentrate so much on the basic principles that an arrangement which sets out to interpret some given subject ends up by being just another lovely design with no real connection with the subject.

A lively yet well-disciplined imagination is the greatest possible asset to the competitive exhibitor.

Take the subject of 'Music'. One arranger interpreted this by means of a rhythmic design, using various white flowers in the form of bells, trumpets, pipes, drums, keys and strings. The leaves of fatsia, with their digital formation, were used to imply that all music comes to life at the command of the human touch. The completed design was staged against a black, accordion-pleated drape, the two colours used, white and black, representing those of the keyboard.

This type of arrangement might not be the wisest choice

for competitive show work as it can be fatal to over-estimate the subtle powers of the hidden meaning.

Commonplace subjects of everyday life sometimes provide the most interesting themes. 'Taking the rough with the smooth' could be interpreted by a design based on the various textures found in wood. A rough twisted piece of driftwood in its natural state placed on a base of highly polished oak or walnut would be most suitable. The use of young roughly wrinkled rhubarb or rodgersia leaves in association with oiled leaves of bergenia or magnolia would emphasize the meaning of the title, and also add considerably to the general effect by virtue of the contrasting colours employed.

Alternatively, the dark brown glossiness of glycerined leaves will combine effectively with the rough texture of dried teasels or artichoke heads.

At a Royal Welsh Show one exhibitor gave a most original interpretation of the subject, 'Tolstoy's "War and Peace" '. A design of lovely 'Peace' roses was very well arranged, and 'War' was cleverly suggested by the trails of bindweed that tightly entwined all the rose stems. The white marble container suggested a sombre note of 'In Memoriam'.

Individuality is something very special, even rare, in floral art these days and it should be appreciated even if one's own personal tastes may rebel against some of the ideas.

'The Spirit of Spring' could be interpreted in three ways:

1. A perfect crescent of willow catkins with five lovely blue iris blooms following the graceful sweep of the outline. A knot of yellow spotted aucuba leaves conceal the pinholder and the whole design is staged on a slab of polished wood. A March hare peeps shyly from behind the design.

2. A beautifully finished triangular design correct in every technical detail. Tulips, irises, freesias and perhaps a lovely spray of clivia for central interest. A choice vase completes this exquisite picture.

3. The base is composed of a piece of moss-covered bark. A few uncurled fern fronds, together with fresh garden daffodils in various stages of growth, are arranged in simple style with their own green leaves. A branch or two of hazel catkins give height to the design. A small knot of primroses and a pair of prancing spring lambs add to the general appeal of this simple picture.

Although Exhibit 3 may possess none of the calculated impact of No. 1 nor the polished sophistication of No. 2, it does truly convey the 'Spirit of Spring'. The bursting of new life is not a calculated, sophisticated matter but a moment of great natural and moving simplicity.

In interpretative work the controversial question is the use of an accessory. It is very important to realize that unless an accessory forms an integral part of the design one should refrain from making a habit of using it simply because it is available. Every accessory used should supplement the spirit or theme and contribute harmonizing colour and texture to the completed design.

In a class where the exhibitor is illustrating the beauty of a piece of fine decorative china it may be advisable to use the piece itself as the focal point of the design, in preference to attempting to repeat the colour, shape and variety of every flower on the china.

For example, a crescent-shaped design of exact-matching golden chrysanthemums and a drape of dull bronze satin makes a pleasing enough picture on an old bronze lustre plate but, obviously, all interest is drawn away from the plate when its beauty is completely over-shadowed by the fresh flowers. Replace the bronze drape by some grey-blue velvet and the lustrous texture of the plate becomes much more apparent. A design of soft downy grey leaves and a single spray of golden autumn berries with a few fronds of bracken is subdued enough not to detract too much from the plate, and supplements the design on the plate with which it harmonizes in colour.

So you will see that the possibilities are endless, but always remember the golden rule: 'To interpret is not to copy.'

The following photographs are examples:
8, 9, 11–21, 30, 46, 68, 80–83, 85, 89–91, 103, 104, 108–112

FLOWER ARRANGEMENT IN CHURCHES

Dorothy Cooke

The arranging of decorations in holy places is a very old tradition. In Leviticus 23, God tells Moses – 'Ye shall keep a feast. And ye shall take you on the first day the boughs of goodly trees and branches of palm trees and the boughs of thick trees and willows of the brook . . . and decorate my tabernacle.' While Isaiah says: 'The glory of Lebanon shall come upon thee, the fir tree, the pine tree and the box together to beautify the place of my sanctuary.'

In ancient times the priests were largely responsible for the decorating of churches but, with the Victorian revival and the encouragement of the laity to take a more active part in the work of the church, gradually it became the custom for ladies to assume responsibility for floral arrangements.

Today church flower arrangers have learnt that 'the art of worship is a combination of all the arts. The experience of faith and the experience of beauty are in some measure identical.' Decorations are planned to be dignified and enhance each architectural detail. The beauty of the flowers can combine with the music and the work of the craftsmen who designed and made the building to create an atmosphere of stillness and worship which induces a quiet receptivity.

Many churches still work to the old and well-beloved tradition of yellow and white flowers for Easter, the yellow symbolizing glory and the white perfection.

At Whitsuntide, red and white decorations are also traditional, the red representing the glorious victory and the tongues of fire that descended at Pentecost.

Arranging flowers for a church should include care and forethought in the preparation and choice of flowers; they should always be freshly cut and not quite in full flower. The stems of branches should be lightly bruised with a hammer before being placed in deep water for a long overnight drink and the stems of the flowers cut.

The positioning of the flowers is a matter of consultation beforehand with the vicar. Many incumbents do not encourage the decorating of the font, for instance. Should it be possible to use a large arrangement, it must look well from all sides. It may be more practical to have the flowers at the base of the font. Long troughs are suitable for this, care must always be taken to ensure that the backs of the arrangements look as well as the fronts. It must be remembered, too, that the flowers will be viewed from above.

To make an arrangement at the base of the font, choose a long earthenware or stone trough and fill this with chicken wire. Place a long piece of foliage at each end and an upright one in the centre twice the length of the container. Gradually fill in this shape with leaves and flowers, placing the smaller flowers on the outside and the larger ones low in the centre. Always allow some flowers and leaves to flow over the rim of the container, on the back as well as the front. If the flowers are arranged on top of the font, follow the instructions for a pedestal arrangement.

For a festival in Victorian times the pulpit was often hung with tins which were filled with flowers and foliage but today, when the pulpit is often handsomely carved in wood or stone, a pedestal arrangement place near by is all that is necessary.

It is very important to consider the design carefully when arranging flowers in large decorations and to see that the contrasting shapes and textures of the plant material are suitably varied and proportioned.

It is customary to make dignified, symmetrical patterns – triangles for example – and these shapes show up well even from the back of a large church. Flowers such as delphiniums and paeonies in the summer and gladioli, dahlias and chrysanthemums in the autumn provide excellent contrasting, bold shapes. For Easter tall flowering branches of forsythia contrast well with lilies and daffodils, while branches of evergreens can add the necessary weight in the heart of the decoration.

For a pedestal at the chancel steps or by the altar choose an upright or urn type of container and fill it with chicken wire. In the centre put a strong main placement of yew, broom, willow or similar foliage twice the height of the container with two side placements one and a half times the height. Fill in with straight and flowing branches to give a pleasant shape but always try to make the stems flow from a central point and allow some to flow forward over the rim of the container. Lilac, delphiniums, larkspur or gladioli are suitable for the taller stems, with lilies, paeonies, roses, carnations, to mention only a few, for the central part. Always have your largest blooms low in the centre. You must take care to see that the pedestal looks well from all angles.

The narrow-necked brass altar vases are the direct descendants of the 'lily vase' of ancient times. They were intended for two or three stems of lilies to be held in the hand and then fastened together to form a vertical pattern leading one's eyes straight to God. If arranged in this way, with the stems in deep water, the flowers will last well for a number of days.

Many churches today do not have flowers on the altar at all but prefer pedestal arrangements at one or both sides of the altar.

The window ledges in churches are often decorated for festivals and weddings. If the windows are of clear glass take care to make a rather more solid shape as sun shining through the flowers can make them almost invisible. If the windows are of dark, stained glass, paler coloured flowers will be found to be more suitable.

Pleasing stone-coloured, boat-shaped vases are easily and cheaply obtainable and so are simple baskets in which a tin may be placed to hold the water.

At Christmas tall white candles set securely in Plasticine among well-cleaned evergreens look very well; and at Easter daffodils massed simply in a row of jars placed along the window ledges and then concealed with moss are easily contrived.

Usually the responsibility does not end with the arranging of the flowers but continues with the replenishment of fresh water and, if necessary, fresh flowers until the agreed time comes to remove them. It is a great help if all the containers are emptied and left clean and ready for the incoming flower arranger.

The following photographs are examples:
22–27

SUMMER FLOWERS

Elsie Lamb

This title conjures up a wealth of colour and profusion in the garden, with herbaceous borders full to over-flowing, arches covered with roses, honeysuckle and clematis, rose beds glowing with colour, tall clumps of foxgloves and a blue haze of lovely delphiniums in the distance. To write briefly about summer flower arrangements with such a wealth of blossom to be found in many English gardens is akin to pouring a quart into a pint pot.

It pays to plan ahead, particularly if there is only a limited garden in which to grow the flowers. Choose colour schemes carefully and try to grow those flowers which will fit in with the décor of the home.

Seed and plant catalogues will prove very rewarding for they give in clear detail all the information required when choosing which plants to grow for flower arranging. The colour, height, period of blooming, hardiness and soil preference of most plants will be stated and in some cases plants suitable for flower arranging are noted. Be sure to choose plants which will grow freely and successfully and will last in full bloom for three or four days in the house.

The majority of women have no time to renew their flowers every day and can only manage a regular 'topping up', a term used to denote the addition of water to a container.

The minimum basic requirements for making a successful flower arrangement are simple and need not entail great expense. Containers, by which anything that will hold water is meant, should relate to the type and colour of the flowers to be used. Crumpled wire netting, usually two-inch mesh, and needlepoint pinholders are often required, also Plasticine or Bostik No. 5 sealing strip to anchor the pinholder when heavy flowers and foliage are used. Water-retaining materials such as Oasis, Florapak or Florafoam are very useful for most flowers but it is advisable to cover them with wire netting. Secateurs or flower scissors, some string, a watering-can with a slender spout for topping up and, last but not least, a sheet of polythene or plastic material to protect the furniture if the flowers are arranged *in situ*.

Simple and effective arrangements using only a few flowers can be made with an interesting piece of driftwood, a pinholder, a shallow tin and a wooden base. This will make the foundation for a successive display of arrangements using summer flowers as they come into bloom. The orange-apricot poppy (*Papaver* 'Mrs Perry') arranged with its own leaves and a piece of wood to hide the pinholder will produce a striking and gay design. The poppies should be picked when just showing colour and, as with all sappy stems, the end must be seared in a flame for a few seconds before standing in cold water. If treated this way the flowers will remain fresh for three or four days. Five stems of the Russell lupin, 'Catherine of York', a lovely apricot yellow, will look arresting with the shiny reddish leaves of bergenia at the base. Three stems of pale blue delphinium, 'Cliveden Beauty', can be arranged with *Hosta sieboldiana* (*H. glauca*), or Gloriosa daisies of rich orange and red colouring with *Bergenia cordifolia* leaves. Roses of all kinds; the vigorous 'Peace' and 'Queen Elizabeth' with their glossy foliage are lovely to look at and easy to arrange.

A large pastel-coloured mass arrangement of pale pink

with green and white can be made by using the fragrant sprays of mock orange (*Philadelphus*) and lime blossoms backed by the white-edged leaves of *Hosta albo-marginata*, four or five stems of *Lilium regale* or *L. longiflorum* and, to give emphasis to the centre, six or seven paeonies, 'Sarah Bernhardt' variety. This elegant design would bring light and fragrance into the corner of a room. The mock orange and lime branches must be defoliated and the ends of the hard stems hammered, placing them in a bucket of water for several hours before the arrangement is made.

There is no other flower which gives greater pleasure in June for a big arrangement than the delphinium. Many people think delphiniums are a nuisance in the house when the petals begin to drop, but if they are picked when opened half-way up the stem and immersed in deep water in a cool place overnight, they will give three or four days of trouble-free beauty. As outline flowers for any arrangement the colour combinations can be endless as the colours range from deep to palest blue, violet-purple to silvery mauve, strawberry pink, white and yellow. The pale pink variety, 'Theodora Parrett', does not drop its petals easily, requires no staking so is well worth growing. A striking and unusual effect can be made in a copper container using grey *Sorbus aria* var. *majestica* and grey artichoke leaves for the outline. Several shorter stems of pinky mauve delphinium, 'Pacific Astolat', for the secondary placements, spikes of red *Monarda didyma* 'Cambridge Scarlet' and the leaves of variegated kale massed in the centre to emphasize the central blooms of crimson paeonies.

A lovely arrangement to bring perfume and tranquillity into a room could be made with long trails of honeysuckle, the round greeny-white heads of *Viburnum opulus sterile*, Regale lilies, pink and white paeonies and pink and white stocks.

Pale blue hydrangeas and delphiniums, some sprays of 'Madame Pierre Oger', a pale pink rose which is sweetly scented and lasts well when cut, with some stems of the yellow-green tobacco plant (*Nicotiana*) arranged in a large alabaster urn or silver wine cooler would make an elegant pedestal arrangement.

For a small arrangement use larkspur laterals, 'Doris' pinks, lime-green *Alchemilla mollis*, mauve and yellow aquilegia, 'Stirling Silver' or 'Magenta' roses with trails of summer jasmine (*J. officinale*). These summer flowers arranged in a small white cherub container would be a great joy.

In summer the wild flowers bloom everywhere in the fields, hedges and woodlands and what is more lovely than an arrangement of wild flowers. Use some spikes of red-green dock seed-heads, rosebay willow herb and foxgloves for the outline. Fill in with stems of red, pink and white valerian, lime-green fennel and the large heads of mauve and white cow parsley, wild spurge and clusters of wild pink and purple rhododendrons in the centre, all backed by red-tinted plantain leaves. Make this arrangement in a large basket with a pie-dish to hold the water. In a cool position it will stay fresh for three or four days provided the stems have been treated in the recommended manner.

A colourful and pleasing overall picture should be your first consideration. With imagination, a basic knowledge of the principles of flower arranging and so many lovely flowers and foliage to choose from, it should not be too difficult to create an outstanding summer flower arrangement.

The following photographs are examples:
11, 31–33, 38

WILD FLOWERS

Patricia Mann

Wild flowers make dainty flower arrangements, and what is more acceptable than a breath of country in the house? Many wild flowers, if treated properly, will last as long as garden flowers; their simple charm and delicacy of colour and texture are without comparison.

When collecting plant material, never pull or break it, and if you are fortunate enough to come across anything that is rare leave it where it is, in order to preserve the species.

It is quite possible the flowers will be out of water for some hours, so it is best to place all plant material directly into a large soft polythene bag dampened inside, keeping it closed as much as possible. Not only will the flowers keep crisp and fresh till you get home but they will also be un-damaged. On arriving home attend to the flowers straight away, carefully sorting out those that do not take up water well. Cover these flower-heads with a soft muslin cloth and hold the bottom half inch of stem in boiling water for a couple of minutes, about half a dozen stems can be done at a time. Then stand all stems in deep water for several hours before arranging them. A simple framework of four garden canes may be made round the sides of the pail with a very large soft polythene bag over the top. This slows down transpiration and helps to draw the water up the stems. This is especially useful when staging at a show overnight. A tent of polythene can be pinned over the arrangement, enveloping it entirely. This is advantageous to all plant material. The plants and flowers to be found growing wild vary, of course, from county to county and it is always exciting to come across something new.

There is a host of wild plants to be found in any type of soil. In February the copse or hedgerow is the best place to look when the first green spikes of the wild arum appear. This plant is useful for its leaves, its curious flower enveloped by a green spathe and, in early autumn, its brightly coloured berries. The leaves last better if totally immersed in water for an hour or so before use. In olden times the root was ground to make starch for the laundress, hence its common name starch-root, but it is also known as lords-and-ladies, or cuckoo-pint. The arum is followed by all the well-known spring flowers, primroses, anemones, violets, celandines, oxalis and pussy willow, which dries well if cut before pollination and hung in bunches. Cowslips, bluebells and sun spurge (*Euphorbia helioscopia*) can be found in April.

The glorious shade of lime-green of the sun spurge is particularly attractive in all types of arrangements. Give it the boiling-water treatment, as it does not take water well, especially after a severe winter. Plants belonging to the Umbelliferae family, such as cow parsley, hogweed, wild carrot, parsnip and angelica, also benefit from this treatment.

Wild carrot and hogweed are very useful at Christmas time when the seeds have dropped, leaving the skeleton umbel. These, sprayed and glittered, are very beautiful. Not so easily found is the angelica with its extremely large heads of greenish-white flowers, which are particularly suitable for pedestal work. Wild parsnip is another lime-green flower, usually growing by the roadside.

Some flowers show a marked preference for chalk soil.

Wild clematis or old man's beard is one; sprays of this plant are useful either fresh or for winter decoration. If cut in the early seed-pod stage and stood in a solution of two parts water to one part glycerine for seven to ten days until the leaves turn brown, they will last indefinitely. Another very colourful plant happy on limestone is viper's bugloss (*Echium vulgare*). This produces three-foot spikes of bright pink buds which turn to clear blue on opening. *Rhododendron ponticum* is often found growing wild on acid soil; this has a very beautiful flower, and is particularly useful in large massed designs.

Many trees provide interesting and useful material. One of the earliest is the Norway maple which bears bunches of lime-green blossoms in early March before the leaves appear. This is followed in April by the very striking white woolly buds of the whitebeam, which on chalk grows into a fine tree but in other situations becomes scarcely more than a shrub. The branches and berries of this tree take a glycerine solution well when the leaves are fully developed, retaining the greyish-white underside to the leaves. Ash bears its curious magenta-coloured blossom in tufts during April before the leaves appear. The lime tree blooms in June, and the branches are most attractive when the leaves have been removed. The flowers can be preserved in glycerine. Look out for *Robinia* (false acacia, as it is sometimes called). Remove some of the leaves and give boiling-water treatment, and the sweetly scented, laburnum-like white flowers will last well. The seeds of hornbeam ripen between very showy pendulous bracts and are to be seen on the underside of the branches all summer; used fresh or glycerined after the leaves have been removed they are most useful.

Later in the summer the common is a happy hunting ground, where the dock and the sorrel turn a glorious shade of coral on the dry exposed hills. Here too grow *Linaria*, wild mignonette, harebells, nettle-leaved bell-flower, rosebay willow herb and various types of heather and ling. Grasses can be found in abundance and are useful for winter decorations. Cut them just as the flower spike emerges from the sheath in June, and hang them upside down in bunches to dry in the dark, and the colour will be retained. The seed-heads of *Linaria*, wild mignonette, bladder campion and St John's wort should be cut in September, while the teasel (*Dipsacus sylvestrii*) should be left to dry out on the plant, and cut about the end of October. The flower spike of the giant reed mace (*Typha latifolia*), commonly called the bulrush, must be cut in June when the spike is green and before pollination, then dried out by standing in a tall jar in the house. Treated in this way it will last for years. If the flower spike of this plant is left till later in the year when it is brown and ripe, it will explode naturally in the spring and be of no further use.

Flower arrangements of any shape or size can be made with wild flowers, from the large pedestal arrangement to the tiniest miniature arrangement, and have a use and appeal equal to those of cultivated flowers.

The following photographs are examples:
21, 28, 29

LINE ARRANGEMENTS

Beryl Ivory

In the simplicity of line arrangements lies their beauty. 'Line' is not meant to be anything hard or anything forced into something that is completely alien to the plant material used. It is making the most of very little material and showing that material at its best.

There are often one or two beautiful blooms in the garden that are a great joy; they may have taken quite skilful growing to reach perfection. If used in a mass arrangement they are lost in the crowd, but arranged with a well-cut branch or interesting piece of driftwood and a few well-chosen leaves they stand out and command admiration.

It is necessary to develop an eye for a line. Think of all the basic shapes: the various triangles, the vertical or the different forms of the crescent and the Hogarth curve. Try to visualize them as outlines into which you are going to place your material.

Look first at your flowers, leaves, branches or driftwood, and choose your main material. See what shape it wants to go of its own free will for this will save much worry, frustration and disappointment. Consider the way it grows, if it is by nature very upright, or if it curves and flows. The growth of the iris, for example, is tall, stately and upright, therefore the choice would be an upright arrangement with straight narrow leaves and fleshy or more rounded ones at the base to give weight. The iris, by its character and texture, lends itself to water, so a design using water as a decorative part can be very pleasing.

Texture is very important. Many line arrangements are bold and dramatic, and this effect is achieved by the use of strong materials, both in weight and colour. Large leaves of exotic appearance, brilliant-coloured tulips in spring, scarlet poppies from the herbaceous border in summer and the oranges and flames of dahlias in the autumn are all suitable. Seed-heads, too, can have dramatic forms and add much to the character of an arrangement. Many quite simple garden or wild plants can look exotic in an arrangement. *Arum italicum*, with its white veining on the leaves, is a good example of this.

One of the most important ingredients of a line design is the choice of material. This requires careful thought and time taken to search for it. Perhaps inspiration has been sparked off by a particularly well-shaped piece of driftwood. What is the right type of flower or leaf to put with it? The plant material in all flower arranging is the main feature and the container should be chosen to display it to greater advantage. Usually it is best to use a plain container but any ornamental or antique container can be used, provided it is in character with the design. If the arrangement is contemporary and dramatic, then the container must have modern lines. A base of any type of material would be suitable for a vertical design such as a rough-cut shape in black glass or white marble, or even natural wood or stone. The container must accentuate the line so that a shallow, narrow-shaped oval or oblong dish with slightly upturned ends could be used for a crescent arrangement and a tall, thin-stemmed container, such as a candle-stick, would be suitable for a Hogarth curve.

Great care must be given to the mechanics of flower

34

arrangement, for if it is not safe and secure disaster and heartache will follow. If a base is used a pinholder in a tin or plastic dish is all that is necessary. The pinholder should be securely anchored with Plasticine or Bostik No. 5. The various ways of securing driftwood are described in the chapter on Driftwood Arrangements. Oasis or similar material can be used for the more flowing and curving type of line, especially when a downward flow is required. Care should be taken that it is not too wet while the arrangement is being made. After the arrangement is completed care should again be taken to see that it is then fully soaked, slowly add more water to the top until it will absorb no more.

Good conditioning of material is essential at all times but more especially with line arrangements. Well matured plant material should always be used. Do not be tempted by that delightful young shoot of delicate colour or that young bud that is too soft of stem, for they cannot take up sufficient water to last and keep their shape.

Continuity of movement is important and it must be possible to follow the line through the arrangement from one point to another. See that the flowers are not placed in a straight line and remember that all three dimensions are as necessary here as anywhere.

To sum up: know your plants well and see that the container and mechanics are suitable, then your line arrangements will be a delight on the show stands or in your home.

The following photographs are examples:
36, 37, 50, 53, 54

PERIOD

Betty Tindall

Flowers arranged in the style of another age can add elegance to a room of contemporary design. This does not always apply; for instance, a vase of flowers arranged in the flamboyant manner of the seventeenth-century Dutch flower painter would not look particularly well with the modern streamline Swedish furnishings. On the other hand, the graceful pastel receding colours of the French eighteenth-century arrangements would suit a room with delicate colouring, mahogany furniture and upholstered chairs. These arrangements, often created by the ladies of the court of Louis XV, were usually composed of exotic flowers and grey foliage with an emphasis on sweetly scented material. The style was an informal triangle with no strong lines but with a gently flowing slightly curved design running from the apex to the rim of the vase, then continuing down one side with heavy-headed flowers and foliage. The vase was a delicate Sèvres or similar porcelain in pastel shades, generally with a brightly coloured flower motif on the front.

The actual flowers used by the court ladies consisted of lilies of all kinds (except arums), stocks, carnations, tulips, French lilac, paeonies, mignonette and masses of Centifolia and Bourbon roses with the grey-green foliage of artemesia and artichoke leaves. To re-create a French flower arrangement of that period the flowers used are all the favourite ones in the present-day summer border. Look

for pale, 'dirty' pinks and mauves. The modern floribunda rose, 'Magenta', together with sweet peas and
freesias and any other suitably coloured blooms and grey
foliage, produces a very realistic French period arrangement in a china or metal urn-type vase.

The boldly designed and baroque arrangements of the
seventeenth-century Dutch painters would be more suitable for halls and dining-rooms where the furnishing
colours are stronger.

These arrangements usually followed an 'S' curve design, which is not always obvious at the first glance.
These still-life pictures showed a composition in which
fruit, insects, birds' nests and various *objets d'art* played a
prominent part in the general design. The colouring
was gay and bright and very mixed. Heavy containers
were used made of terracotta, glass or metal and always
heavily embossed. The flowers were in great variety,
nearly all of which are in common cultivation today.

All the spring-flowering bulbs were used, tulips pre-
dominating, also auriculas, polyanthus, paeonies, poppies,
marigolds, roses, lilies and many others.

Use a little ingenuity when collecting the flowers to
make a Dutch arrangement, and the wonderful variety will
surprise you. Look for the correct colouring and shapes of
the flowers rather than the true kinds used by the painters.
It is fun to try and find flowers that are flowering out of
season as this was the great trick of the Dutch masters.
They painted in summer blooms later to the original composition of spring flowers. Search for late tulips, both
double and single, early paeonies (tree variety), early
'China' or 'Monthly' roses, irises, Spanish cultivated bluebells and any similar material that is available. The foliage
does not present any difficulty as good firm curving stems
are used for outlines, honeysuckle, jasmine or forsythia

sprays are ideal. Poppy, paeony and bergenia leaves are equally suitable for the background.

Remember to use brilliant colours, blending them in with lime-green and touches of white. Be as daring as you like with apparently clashing colours; the result will be delightful and not nearly as difficult to achieve as you may imagine.

Victorian-style decorations need a little care. The flower arrangements of the nineteenth century generally do not appeal to present-day tastes. They were in the main heavy, shapeless and without any real colour scheme. Victorian-style decorations need a little more care to make. Many are charming and would look lovely in a country house drawing-room with its chintz-covered chairs, Victorian furniture and old china.

Many double and striped flowers were used as it was the fashion then to despise single varieties. The foliage consisted of small-leaved ivies or ferns, often no greenery was used at all. Vases of all kinds were used, and nearly all were highly ornamented.

There is one other period of flower arrangement about which I can say very little because, strictly speaking, it did not exist in real life. I am, of course, referring to the Regency period, which was a time of elegance and flamboyance in interior decoration and furnishings. There was some flower arrangement and flowers were used to decorate the dining table. It is, however, not sufficiently defined to single out as a distinct period of floral art. It was essentially the era of the potted plant; life was very arduous for the women of the day and there was little leisure time to spend in arranging flowers.

To make an arrangement to harmonize with a Regency room, use any elegant flowers in a bold design, such as lilies, paeonies and pale full-blown roses. There is, of course, a clearly defined Regency container which was used to hold the various flowering potted plants and palms. It is shaped like a large egg-cup and made of mahogany and is sometimes copied in pottery today. The elaborate silver wine coolers of the time also make excellent vases for this type of decoration.

Try some period arrangements in your home. There are not many houses where they would look out of place, they are immensely satisfactory when finished and are the greatest fun to do.

The following photographs are examples:
59–63

DRIFTWOOD ARRANGEMENTS

Marian Aaronson

Wood that has been weathered by the natural elements of wind, sun or water becomes a thing of beauty. It is used today by flower arrangers because it has many attributes to make a design more arresting or beautiful. They have become avid collectors, combing the beaches, mountain tops, woods and streams for treasures. The search that starts as fun soon becomes a serious occupation. The findings vary and are not always spectacular but once in a while a really beautiful piece awaits the diligent searcher.

Different pieces will be valued for their own special qualities – a lovely texture, intriguing shape or interesting colour. The wood from the seashore has perhaps the finest texture, its roughness worn smooth by the waves and stones, the salt water and sun bleaching it silvery white.

The forest may yield tree roots and knobbly bark, a rougher, coarser texture, the colour being varied and interesting. The twisted stems of ivy are particularly beautiful.

Interesting pieces are found on the high mountain, silver-grey and smooth, bent and twisted in a pitiless fashion by the wind and rain to form an object of rugged grandeur. Pieces of gorse are found on exposed sites, bent almost double by the force of the wind and often blackened by fire. These pieces would lend themselves to a dramatic composition or interpretative arrangement.

Each piece of driftwood should be studied to discover

its potentialities. One may suggest a windswept movement, another may look like a bird or animal. Some are so distinctive that they become an ornament to be displayed like a piece of fine sculpture. Each piece is unique and will never be seen elsewhere.

Driftwood makes a good foil for brilliant flowers and leaves, their brightness being intensified by contrast with the mellow, subdued hues of the wood. It blends equally well with the quieter colours of dried plant material, producing harmonies and pleasing designs when flowers are scarce and expensive. A basic design of driftwood will last and retain interest for many months with a few flowers and leaves which can be changed when necessary, thus conserving time and energy.

Driftwood is bold and dominant and can often be used in a daring and dramatic manner to interpret a theme or mood. Used like this it has sufficient impact to give the vital spark that kindles the imagination.

Driftwood probably looks best when left in its natural state. The hand of nature blends colours admirably, but very attractive results can be obtained with cleaning, bleaching, polishing or staining. Liquid wax rubbed into the surface produces a soft sheen, and brown boot polish gives a rich finish. Staining with a wood dye will change the colour, giving distinction to the odd piece. A coat of varnish will give a glossy surface, vegetable dyes brushed over the wood give a surprisingly attractive appearance, while the green sap from fleshy leaves will increase the colour interest. It is better to try out the results on less valued pieces before altering for ever the more precious pieces.

Pruning is often necessary to improve the general shape, and it is advisable to remove or scrape out any sections which are soft or rotting. Soaking in a strong disinfectant and antiseptic solution is a wise precaution before bringing the wood indoors.

Good mechanics are essential when using driftwood, for a large piece cannot stand without adequate support. Heavy, bulky pieces are best trimmed flat at the base and screwed into a flat piece of wood; a pinholder and a dish for the plant material resting on this will give additional balance. A jagged piece of wood can be set in a pyramid of Polyfilla which, when set, becomes self-supporting, and can be anchored in position with a piece of Plasticine. Soft pieces can be impaled straight on to a strong pinholder, but if the wood is hard drill a few holes into the base and insert short pieces of wood, which will fix straight on to the pinholder. If there is no water in the container, light pieces of wood can be fixed with a ball of Plasticine. This must be hidden with the leaves and flowers at the base of the arrangement. Always remember that the flowers must not obliterate the driftwood. The one must complement the other.

Many beautiful driftwood arrangements are seen at the flower arrangement shows and exhibitions; they also fit well into our homes. The beauty of the wood blends with any style or type of setting and the mellow colouring is soothing to the eye and easy to live with.

The following photographs are examples:
64, 65, 68–71, 115, 117

AUTUMN FLOWERS

Adèle Gotobed

September brings the shortening days and morning mists, it is a time when cobwebs sparkle like fabulous pearl-studded jewels linked as necklaces from plant to plant. Heavy dew covers the ground and the garden is full of flowers: dahlias, early chrysanthemums, michaelmas daisies, roses, lilies, seed-heads, foliage, vines, fruits and vegetables. With so much to choose from, it is difficult to decide what to select for a flower arrangement. Do not get carried away with the splendour of the blooms or colours, as too much of everything will spoil the effect of the finished design. For those who have the space, this is the season for making mass and pedestal arrangements.

Most of the autumn material is heavy in weight and texture and of strong colour, lending itself to bold treatment. Containers must be equally heavy and bold. All the metals seem ideal, such as bronze urns and figurines that have been adapted into containers, copper and brass trays and jugs, pewter dishes, plates and other metal vessels. Lovely alabaster vases and containers made of wood are also suitable, but they must be lined with metal.

Materials grow stronger with age, and many leaves that prove difficult to keep turgid in summer stand up very well in the autumn, but naturally they all require conditioning with a good drink before being arranged. Ferns respond very well when they are mature, as do some of the grey leaves. It is always wise to put the stems (about one inch) in hot water for a few minutes before giving them a long drink of cold water.

Autumn includes the Harvest Festival and many arrangers are called upon to do the festival flowers for the church. There is usually a good supply of material which will need sorting into colours, tall spiky stems, round flowers, and trailing stems such as vines and ivy which are useful for pedestal arrangements. Group the white, yellow, flame and coppery colours together and the mauves, greys and reds in another place. Corn and grasses mingle beautifully in most harvest arrangements, and if the corn is tied in small bunches it will be easier to handle and will be more clearly seen at a distance. If possible arrange the fruit and vegetables in baskets; these can be linked by colour or foliage to the pedestal groups. In this way damage to the fruits and vegetables will be avoided, and distribution will be easier afterwards.

Autumn is the time of fulfilment. The beautiful flame, purple and red colours abound, everything tries to give of its best in a final fling to produce the seeds for another year, and it is a good time to take stock for the future flower arrangement needs. A walk in the local park or a visit to a large garden or nursery can provide first-hand knowledge of how to group plants together to improve the colour harmony in the garden, and what to grow for flower arranging.

It is always a good thing to grow something different each year, as it is easy to get into a rut with old favourites. Where space is limited it may be prudent to concentrate on growing foliage. Some which are useful for autumn decoration are the various Barberries, *Berberis thunbergii*, *B. polyantha* and *B. thunbergii atropurpurea*; these give long sprays, frequently covered with lovely berries, which are so useful for the outline of an arrangement when many round flowers abound. *Cotoneaster horizontalis* is lovely when used sparingly with bright red dahlias and bergenia leaves.

There are several varieties of *Rhus*, some with dull reddish leaves, and others with purple. Sprays of 'Notcutts' variety are useful for a centre interest, blending in well with many colour schemes. The foliage of vines is also most useful and some varieties give fruit as well. The mature leaves last well if given a good drink. The green leaves of *Vitis vinifera* 'Brandt' turn to lovely honey and autumn colours; it has small fruit which turn from green to purple. *Vitis vinifera* var. *purpurea* has smaller leaves of a reddish-purple hue, which are ideal as trails for large arrangements, and for use in conjunction with flowers and fruits.

Berries abound in the autumn; *Callicarpa giraldiana* has lovely purple berries and is very prolific, but only if two or three are planted together and the leaves are attractive, taking on a purple hue. It is, however, at its best when the leaves have fallen.

An attractive arrangement can be made in a large pewter dish by using ornamental kale for the outline and choosing leaves that have taken on an attractive yellow edge. These will blend with sprays of yellow-orange berries from a rambler rose and longish sprays of *Callicarpa*. Carry *Rhus* leaves through the centre of the arrangement, and over the front of the container. Fill it with green and yellow peppers (*Capsicum*), gourds and green grapes. There are usually a few roses in bloom late in the year, which could be used in place of the fruit. The floribunda 'Magenta' is lovely, coupled with any pale yellow roses, or as an alternative use dahlias or spray chrysanthemums.

Another autumn grouping which can be compiled in a large work box consists of *Berberis atropurpurea* and *Berberis polyantha* (lovely green flushed berries), *Kniphofia* in yellow flame to orange colourings, seed-heads of *Astilbe*, paeony foliage, with yellow tomatoes and sprays of small decorative tomatoes.

'Rayonante' chrysanthemums can be obtained from florists in pastel colours which are lovely in mixed flower groups but perhaps look their best when arranged alone. They combine beautifully with some of the lovely sculptured driftwood so popular with flower arrangers today.

It is fortunate that all flower arrangers have different tastes so that each arrangement can have individuality. With so many combinations of colour and material available, autumn flower arrangements are fun to create and a joy to behold.

The following photographs are examples:
72, 73

MINIATURE ARRANGEMENTS

Peggy Lovell

Let 'scale' be the watchword for ever ringing in your ears when doing a small arrangement; it is the essence of every miniature arrangement. Every flower arrangement must be to scale but the big difference with the small arrangement is that the margin of error is so infinitesimal that a mere eighth of an inch on a leaf can ruin the whole effect.

Some people think miniatures hardly count as flower arrangements, yet at a show they invariably attract the most interest from the general public. Although these arrangements are associated mainly with the shows and competitions, a tiny vase of flowers on a mantelshelf or among smaller pieces of old china will enhance any home.

Neat, but not necessarily small, fingers are needed for making a miniature arrangement and strong spectacles plus a magnifying glass, eyebrow tweezers, stub wire or a compass point and a small quantity of Oasis, Florapak or similar material. Condition your plant material and carry it to the show in water then, when complete, top up with an eye dropper or syringe.

Most important of all is a suitable container. There is no need to search in the junk shops for a tiny container; the freshly painted top of a tube or bottle, a thimble mounted on a tiny base, something from a doll's house, or sometimes a toy from a Christmas cracker would be suitable. Home-made containers modelled from Plasticine and painted the required colour are ideal. Buttons make splendid bases, but beware of spoiling a really lovely miniature with a base that is too heavy. Scale, again remember, is the watchword.

As in all flower arranging, it can be the container that gives the first idea from which to create a design; or the plant material may guide the choice of the colour scheme.

The actual planning and subsequent arranging of the little masterpiece is the same as for a larger arrangement. Any shape is possible: the triangle, the crescent, the Hogarth curve or the upright. A miniature composition with the tiniest china figurine, piece of driftwood or drape is a real joy. The overall measurement of a true miniature is four inches, so, always remembering the word 'scale', use twists of fuse wire instead of the usual chicken wire.

If you are entering a miniature at a show, it is wise to take along quite a few spare pieces for the stem of your tallest bud can easily break off or a tiny petal can become damaged. Try to use plant material that will last well, especially if it is a two-day show.

In the rock garden much suitable dwarf material is easily available. Miniatures require such tiny snippets from plants that it is easy to beg from friends who often give a free hand to pick what is needed without any worry of their garden being stripped of precious things.

The following is a list of plants that are useful to grow for miniature arrangements, but only the smallest of leaves and buds are suitable even from these:

1 Tiny succulents of all colours.
2 *Lonicera japonica* var. *aureo reticulata*.
3 Ferns (each sideshoot a miniature fern in itself).
4 Grasses (wild types take the place of bulrushes).
5 Ivy (*Hedera conglomerata* and *H. sagittaefolia*).

6   *Dianthus* (mock iris leaves for outline).
7   Geranium (the leaves of 'Mrs Henry Cox', 'Caroline Smith' and 'L'Elegant').
8   *Anaphalis* (white everlasting flower).
9   *Cyclamen neopolitanum* (marbled foliage).
10   *Iris cristata* and *I. lacustris* (under three inches high).
11   *Tunica saxifraga* (like a minute pink carnation).
12   *Lapeyrousia cruenta* (rock bulb-like gladiolus).
14   *Maianthemum bifolium* (mock lily of the valley).
14   Roses in miniature varieties ('Peon', 'Pumila', etc.).
15   *Salix repens* (creeping willow).
16   *Oxalis adenophylla* (grey fan-like leaves).

The following photographs are examples:
76–79

FOLIAGE ARRANGEMENTS

Dorothy Tuffin

Foliage when correctly used will enhance almost any flowers. It will act as a foil and a few well-placed leaves of *Begonia rex*, croton or *Dracaena* can lift the most mundane arrangement out of its dullness. Leaves can be used by themselves very effectively when flowers are not available. It is important to select foliage with great care as a combination of leaves does not necessarily produce a pleasant effect and certain types of leaves tend to produce great confusion when massed together.

Colour plays as important a part in a foliage arrangement as with a flower arrangement, so aim to get a similar effect with leaves. Variegated foliages are invaluable for light shades and for the darkest shades use glycerized foliages. It is a good idea to keep a pot containing a solution of one part glycerine and two parts water always ready. Put any interesting foliage in this for three weeks adding more glycerine and water when necessary. Euonymus, Spanish chestnut, laurel, camellia, bergenia and ivy are a few of the many kinds of foliage worth treating in this way.

The beginner often makes the mistake of attempting to use too many varieties in an arrangement and does not do enough pruning beforehand. It is best to use only four or five types in a first foliage arrangement.

For a simple arrangement choose a piece of wood or a pewter plate for the base. Place a tin on it containing a pinholder covered with a small piece of chicken wire.

Choose a spiky foliage for the outline, such as yucca or broom – strengthen this with privet, fern or *Skimmia*. Next add bolder leaves such as *Fatsia*, laurel or bergenia and finally add a group of leaves with colour to give interest. This could be *Tellima*, curly kale or a succulent such as *Echeveria*.

An asymmetrical triangle design which would stand for many weeks could be made as follows: place a few spiky leaves of yucca or New Zealand flax (*Phormium tenax variegatum*) then a transition material of golden privet or ivy, next *Fatsia* or bergenia to give weight. The interesting marbled leaves of *Arum italicum marmoratum* would make a good centre. A few lemons could be added in winter or daffodils in spring to give a little variation. For a mass effect use a bronze or black urn. The foliage chosen would entirely depend on the time of the year but in October, when the glorious autumn colouring is so beautiful, sprays of beech could form the outline, care being taken to thin the branches if they are too heavy. The next placement could be either golden privet or *Elaeagnus* with some slightly larger foliage to follow. Spanish chestnut, or possibly *Skimmia*, would be suitable. Use a contrast of colour to form the centre of interest, which could be varied and changed from time to time depending on what was available – some *Mahonia japonica* leaves, bergenia, the pinky mauve rosettes from the tips of elder from the hedgerows or the centre of ornamental kale.

The Hogarth curve is a design which lends itself to foliage arrangements. Use a pedestal type of container and create the outline with groups of broom. Gentle massage will easily coax these into shape. For the second placement use *Mahonia japonica* and fill in towards the centre with *Ballota* or rhododendron. Finish with a piece of aucuba laurel or for extra colour use ornamental kale.

51

A plant table near a window in the kitchen is ideal for growing *Sanseviera*, croton, *Aphelandra*, *Begonia rex* and other plants with useful foliage which enjoy the warm steamy conditions of a kitchen.

The smallest garden, by careful planning, can have foliage readily available all the year round and with correct grouping, excellent effects can be produced in a garden of any size. Groups of *Iris pseudacorus variegata*, *Hosta fortunei* 'Albo Picta' and *Euphorbia epithymoides* makes a wonderful splash of acid-green and yellow and give delight for at least two months when the colours gradually dull to darker green and continue until late summer. Another attractive grouping is *Mahonia japonica*, Japanese laurel (*Aucuba japonica*), *Elaeagnus pungens* and ivy (*Hedera canariensis*) growing against a pine tree. Slender New Zealand flax, with the dull rich green of rosemary and *Rhus*, the grey of *Artemisia lactiflora* 'Silver Queen' and the rich purple of *Berberis thunbergii atropurpurea*, make a most unusual grouping.

The following is a list of shrubs and plants useful to the flower arranger, most of which are easy to grow in the garden.

SHRUBS

Berberis thunbergii var. *atropurpurea*
Cupressus macrocarpa var. *lutea*
Cytisus (broom)
Ligustrum ovalifolium var. *aureo-marginatum* (golden privet)
Mahonia japonica
Pieris formosa var. *forrestii*, 'Wakehurst' variety
Rhus cortinus foliis purpureus
Rosa rubrifolia
Skimmia japonica
Viburnum rhytidophyllum

COLOURED AUTUMN FOLIAGE

Bergenia cordifolia
Canna
Enkianthus campanulatus
Euonymus europaeus (spindle tree)
Ferns, various
Fothergillia monticola
Parrotia persica
Polygonatum multiflorum (solomon's seal)
Rhododendron luteum
Rhododendron, Knap Hill hybrids
Tellima grandiflora purpurea
Yucca

GREY PLANTS

Anaphalis triplenervis
Artemisia lactiflora 'Silver Queen'
Cynara cardunculus (cardoon)
Senecio cineraria 'White Diamond'
Senecio laxiflolius
Stachys lanata
Verbascum bombyciferum var. *broussa*

VARIEGATED FOLIAGE PLANTS AVAILABLE IN SPRING

Arum italicum
Aucuba japonica maculata
Camellia
Elaeagnus pungens
Euonymus japonicus aureus
Euphorbia epithymoides
Hedera canariensis 'Gloire de Marengo' (Ivy)
Hosa fortunei 'Albo Picta'

Hosta lancifolia
Iris pseudacorus variegatum
Ilex aquifolium 'Golden King' (holly)
Ilex aquifolium 'Silver Queen' (holly)
Phormium tenax variegatum

The following photographs are examples:
84, 87, 89–91

POT-ET-FLEUR

Edith R. Wise

When Miss Violet Stevenson wrote of this type of arrangement in one of our leading daily papers in 1960, she was agreeably surprised at the interest it aroused. During the following year The National Association of Flower Arrangement Societies in their National Competitions at the Royal Horticultural Society included a class for *Pot-et-fleur*. The wording of the Schedule is not without interest:

'An arrangement of growing plants in or ex pots, and cut flowers assembled in one basic container with bark, driftwood, rock and similar natural accessories at exhibitor's discretion.'

This definition fully described this attractive style of arrangement. To this class, the Flowers and Plants Council awarded a challenge cup. Thus *Pot-et-fleur* was born. The class presents a challenge, and many attractive presentations of this style are seen at shows.

Pot-et-fleur can be explained quite simply: Living plants are placed in a container. Cut flowers complementary to the foliage are then arranged within this outline. Plants can be graded into three types, tall, shrubby and hanging. Choose about five plants for a grouping, for they enjoy living in a community. Cover the bottom of the selected container with stones or crocks to which has been added a little crushed charcoal, then partially fill with John Innes No. 1 potting compost. Remove the selected plants from their pots and carefully plant them in the container, easing more compost around the roots where necessary. Do not overcrowd but take great care to arrange the living plants into a good basic shape, selecting them for their contrasting shapes, textures and colours. Driftwood fits very naturally into this type of arrangement. It can give height and is also very useful for the support of climbing plants.

Flowers are inserted into cone holders which are carefully hidden behind the plants; a container of a few selected plants is thus transformed into a colourful *Pot-et-fleur* arrangement.

Another method is to leave the plants in their pots and sink them in moistened peat to the rims. Keep the peat damp. The humidity thus created is appreciated by most plants whose worst enemy is the dry atmosphere within a room. Plants thus arranged look particularly well in copper preserving pans, soup tureens etc.

In towns where foliage is rather a problem, it is pleasant to have growing greenery within the house, only awaiting the addition of a few flowers.

An effective line arrangement can be achieved by placing pot plants within, and to one side of, a large shallow dish. These should be stood on a small platform of stones to keep them above water-level. Driftwood will hide the pots and add charm to the arrangement, which can be dressed with flowers suitable for a water scene.

Attractive *Pot-et-fleur* arrangements of a more temporary nature can be obtained by removing plants from their pots, and placing them in small plastic bags. This method is more convenient for competitive work where transportation can be a problem.

A word of warning to the compilers of competitive schedules. Keep the requirements small or you may be surprised to see your competitors arriving complete with plants, trowel, etc., and even pushing a wheelbarrow.

The following plants are among those suitable for a *Pot-et-fleur* arrangement:

Decorative ivies
Fatshedera
Philodendron scandens
Tradescantia
Zebrina pendula
Peperomia
Begonia rex
Chlorophytum
Coleus
Sansevieria

There are, of course, many more. You will find that some plants seem easier to grow than others; so make your own selection and you will find that *Pot-et-fleur* arranging will, with practice, become most rewarding.

The following photographs are examples:
115–118

DRIED ARRANGEMENTS

Sylvia Pullan

At this time of the year, when the flowers are disappearing from our gardens, how useful it is to have some dried or preserved material to use, not merely as a substitute for fresh flowers, but for the delicate beauty of colour and form that well-prepared dried flowers and foliage can show. And now it is the time to look for many kinds of material that can be painted and glittered for Christmas arrangements. The seed-heads, cones, leaves and flowers that are to be preserved must be collected throughout the year, each to be taken at the right time. Most flowers should be picked young, almost as soon as they are open, although there are some exceptions such as hydrangeas and achillea. They usually take two or three weeks to dry.

Seed-heads and everlasting flowers are easily dealt with. Tie them in bunches and hang them upside down to dry in a dark, airy place; but useful curves can sometimes be obtained in stalks and branches by drying the material upright in a vase or bottle, allowing the stems to bend over naturally.

Dried flowers lack the light-reflecting quality of fresh ones but the pleasant mellow tones of brown, buff, fawn and grey are often appreciated and it is possible to obtain quite colourful results. Everlasting flowers especially give bright colours, for example *Helichrysum* (yellow, orange, red, pink and white), *Acroclinium* and *Rhodanthe* (pink and white), *Xeranthemum* (mauve and white) and *Statice* (pink, blue, mauve and yellow).

It is advisable to pass a hooked stub wire through the central disc of most flower heads as soon as they are picked (first removing the stalks) as the dried stalks reabsorb moisture from the atmosphere, causing the flower heads to droop. The stub wire itself can be hidden by passing it through the hollow stem of dried grass, poppy, larkspur, iris, etc., giving the appearance of a real stalk.

Delphinium, *Liatris*, larkspur and *Amaranthus hypo-chondricus* are but a few of the flowers that can be dried successfully by hanging them up in bunches. Hydrangeas, whose lovely tonings of blue, mauve, red and green are so very useful, are best left to dry naturally standing in water, but they can be gathered from the plants when crisp to the touch and then hung up in bunches to finish off.

Many leaves are best preserved with glycerine. Make a solution of one part of glycerine and two of hot water. Hammer the stem of the branches to be preserved and stand the ends in two or three inches of the mixture while it is still warm, then leave for two or three weeks. Material preserved in this way has the advantage of being pliable and so is less likely to break. The individual leaves keep their natural positions, giving a three-dimensional effect to an arrangement. August and September are good months for using the glycerine method but experiments can be made with leaves picked at different times. The younger leaves become lighter in colour; the more mature they are the darker the colour obtained.

A collection of dried leaves should include both large and small, solid-looking ones, like laurel and magnolia, and graceful fernlike ones. The bright autumn colours of leaves such as sumach, maple and some cherries add their red and orange to the quieter green, brown and grey of others.

Leaves preserved in glycerine are often suitable for painting and glittering for Christmas but they acquire a greasy surface and whitening tends to peel off. In this case, try a plastic-based paint instead.

A surprising variety of flowers retain their colour and form beautifully if preserved in powdered alum or borax. They must be absolutely free from moisture, such as rain or dew, before they are treated or they will not keep. The base of a box or dish is covered with a layer of the powder, which may be alum or borax or a mixture of the two. The flowers are placed on this and gently sprinkled with the rest of the powder until they are completely covered, the petals being carefully smoothed out if necessary. The full box is kept in a hot cupboard and a week should be long enough to complete the drying process. If the flowers are not ready when examined replace them, but great care will be necessary. Larger flowers may need as long as two or three weeks; if the flowers are left too long, however, there is a danger that they will disintegrate. The powder may need to be sieved if used a second time.

Zinnias, roses, dahlias, sunflowers, snowdrops, narcissi, etc., can all be dried successfully by this method; but frail textured flowers such as sweet peas are not good subjects. The finished material can be stored in boxes and will keep indefinitely if stored in a dry place. Arrangements of material dried in this way tend to absorb moisture from the atmosphere if they are left too long.

Granular silica gel could be used to preserve more robust foliage. It is not dear to buy and is very effective. Fine sand which has been thoroughly dried in an oven could also be used but both these substances are too coarse and heavy for delicate flowers.

Certain 'woody' fungi and lichens can be dried naturally in a warm place and are useful additions to a collection.

If more than one or two boxes of dried specimens are to be kept it is essential to label them systematically so that the contents of each is immediately clear.

Wall plaques of dried material are becoming popular and can be very attractive. For these you need a base of wood, hardboard, matting or other suitable material, the colour contrasting with the arrangement or making a neutral background. For smallish arrangements it may be sufficient to fix the dried leaves and flowers to the base by using a suitable adhesive but for anything at all heavy a thread of fine wire will be necessary. Drill the holes needed for threading the wire before beginning the arrangement.

Plaques can be framed to make very attractive pictures, and smaller ones can be used as Christmas calendars to send to friends or to sell at bazaars.

If any dried stems are to stand in water, for example when used with fresh flowers, it is essential to coat them with shellac or nail varnish, otherwise they will soon begin to soften and rot.

Much of the material needed for dried arrangements can be obtained from a normal garden but even with no garden it is possible to collect a great variety of specimens from woods, wayside or seashore. Driftwood and pieces of bark of interesting shape, colour and texture, when thoroughly dried, harmonize well with dried flowers, fruit and leaves.

In addition to natural grasses it is now possible to buy seeds of ornamental varieties which grow easily in a garden, and a handful of mixed corn will provide plenty of wheat, barley and oats. Indian corn or maize (*Zea mays* or

Japanese maize) will give useful male 'flowers' as well as the cobs and leaves. Grevillea and eucalyptus seed-heads are now obtainable from florists.

A new and exciting development is the recent appearance in this country of unusual seed-heads and dried fruits from warmer countries such as South Africa, and many florists have supplies from time to time.

If first efforts at drying material are not always successful do not be discouraged. Everyone has to experiment and so learns to appreciate the beauties of shape and colour in seeking the best ways of preserving the flowers and foliage.

The following photographs are examples:
18, 19, 46, 50, 51, 76, 77, 80, 85–88, 92–101, 107, 109, 113

CHRISTMAS ARRANGEMENTS

Margaret Couper

The Christmas festival affords opportunities for the intro-
duction of themes and the use of materials not legitimately
permissible at any other time of year. At this season flower
arrangers can give full scope to their ingenuity by experi-
menting with fresh and preserved evergreens, gilded
leaves, pine cones, ribbons, artificial materials, sparkling
baubles and candles; these all help to bring warmth and
colour into our homes.

The traditional use of evergreens, with or without
berries, is still, and I hope always will be, the main theme
in Christmas decorations. The important thing is to decide
in advance the appropriate places to decorate, and to
choose materials and colours that best suit the character
and décor of your home, bearing in mind that fresh
flowers and painted or artificial materials are difficult to
combine successfully.

Artificial materials should be used with great care. The
same basic principles of design, scale and harmony apply
to Christmas decorations as to fresh arrangements; fine
pointed materials to the outside, with weight to the centre
of the design.

When planning arrangements remember that they will
have to stand for at least two weeks and should be firmly
anchored; pinholders and wire netting must be used for
heavy fresh materials, Oasis can be used for lighter materials.
Plasticine is ideal for most artificial and dried materials.

Christmas dinner tables should be gay and colourful, and need extra special attention. Use more colour than usual and be bold with your design. Scarlet, green and gold are always effective colourings to use. Even without flowers at this time of year attractive table arrangements can be made using Styrofoam as a base. This is a strong plastic substance which can be cut to any shape by using a hot knife. Plasticine wired on to it will hold evergreens, candles and baubles in position. When Styrofoam is used alone as a base all materials must be wired to penetrate it. If used in a container it can be fastened down by Plasticine or melted wax.

To make a gay, inexpensive evergreen garland for a wall, side-table or mantelshelf use clippings of holly, box and cedar and tie in small bunches with green garden twine or fine wire to a heavy green cord, or a length of thick wire covered with florist's tape.

Start at centre of the cord or wire working outwards, so that the evergreens fall in opposite directions. At intervals between the foliage add lightly gilded cones, wax Christmas roses and small scarlet and green baubles. If it is required for a side-table or mantelshelf, the garland can be attached to candle-sticks with wires and Plasticine. Finish off the ends with bows of scarlet Silsheen ribbon and use with tall dark green candles.

Before painting or glittering do any wiring that may be required to lengthen or strengthen stems, use stub wires or hollow plant stems, then the wires and materials can all be painted at the same time.

Striking effects can be achieved, also brush marks and globules avoided, by using spray paints in gold, silver and copper. One application should be sufficient but remember to cover completely both sides of the materials. A charming effect can be obtained by using copper and silver together. Other interesting colour schemes can be made by painting materials with iridescent powder paints which come in a wide variety of shades and can be bought by the ounce. Try using bronze with moss-green, red with gold, blue or lilac with silver.

Natural materials such as *Mahonia japonica*, aspidistra, ivy, laurel, etc., will last for many months if covered with either hairspray or Polybond before being gilded. Beautiful results can be attained by lightly gilding dried or preserved materials so that the natural fawns and browns of the materials are shown.

To whiten large quantities of foliage and seed-heads, mix a bucketful of washable distemper to a creamlike consistency, dip the materials and allow them to drip dry.

Fragile materials such as skeletonized magnolia leaves must be painted separately. Use flat white paint or shoe white; the latter gives good results, but is not such an effective seal as paint. It has the advantage that it can be washed off the materials, and so they can be used again in their natural state.

To apply glitter, cover the required materials lightly with gum or nail varnish, using a small brush or sponge for quick results. Place the glitter in an old pepper pot, and sprinkle surfaces liberally, allowing any surplus to fall on clean paper for future use.

Old baubles can be given a new lease of life by being lightly painted with gum, then sprinkled with glitter.

Used with restraint, glitter can impart a magical touch to Christmas decorations. It is now possible to buy untarnishable glitter so that materials can be stored and used again another year.

Cones can be opened and made more decorative by placing in a warm oven for a few hours. To add stems, ease a wire between the scales of the lower portion of the cone, leaving equal lengths of wire on each side, then twist together to make the stem.

To prevent pine needles and holly from dropping, paint the branches with clear varnish, Polybond or hairspray.

To prolong the life of newly cut branches or evergreens, place them in a weak solution of five parts hot water to one part glycerine for a few hours.

Evergreens can also be kept fresh by sticking the stems in raw potatoes wrapped in aluminium foil.

When leaves of aspidistra are being dried for Christmas arrangements, they can be set in graceful curves by taping wire on the back, along the spine, then bending them into interesting shapes.

In planning the decoration of your home always remember that a few large arrangements, strategically placed, are infinitely better than numerous small decorations scattered around the home. Remember also that the majority of materials used at Christmas time are highly inflammable, and great care should be taken especially when using candles.

The following photographs are examples:
49, 108–114

THE ART OF JAPANESE
FLOWER ARRANGEMENT

Maud Cole

The impact of this stimulating and satisfying art was first
felt in this country in 1953 when Stella Coe demonstrated
how branches, flowers and leaves arranged in the Japanese
manner can be applied to western homes. We were intro-
duced to such magical words as Moribana, Nageire,
kenzan, jushis and tome.

At first, those of us who were practising western flower
arrangement felt confusion at the completely different use
and purpose to which flowers were put. It was not long,
however, before we realized that here was a great opportunity for expression and also a way to relax and tran-
quillize the mind. Soon we learnt restraint, patience and
humility as taught by nature, for the Japanese identify
themselves much more closely with nature than Euro-
peans seem to do. We have learnt through the years that
Japanese flower arrangements are not 'impact' designs
but, instead, the more they are contemplated the more
satisfying they become.

The basic factor in this type of arrangement is the position of the three levels or planes known as 'Heaven, Man
and Earth', or to give them their Japanese names – Shin,
Soe and Hikae – whose deeper meaning is one of Spiritual
Truth, Man the Harmonizer and Material Substance.
These three lines are set at varying degrees from an
imaginary zero line which is vertical. Their positions vary
in each type of design, for example, in an upright design

or a windswept design. These types of design can be modified. Line is all-important; pruning takes place in order to reveal line and encourage a feeling of movement or to eliminate the congestion of leaves. Not only do we learn to handle and present each living part to its best advantage but also to regard stones, shells and other things as living too.

We learn how to manipulate branches, bending or twisting them gently to improve or complete a line. Flowers are not placed looking directly to the front, the Japanese consider this 'rude'; they turn their flowers a little to right or left. Leaves are used at the base of the arrangement to create a feeling of natural growth and here is the essence of Japanese flower arrangement 'that the plant material is not just arranged but is living in the container'. To this end, in England we often use roots, stones, bark or shells to hide the pinholder (kenzan), but even this is not encouraged in some 'schools'. There are many schools of Japanese flower arrangement and some have adapted the classical or Seika style to suit the modern setting, but it is safe to say that the three levels or planes are common to all of them. It is generally accepted that, provided the kenzan is not obvious when the arrangement is viewed from three feet, it is not necessary to conceal it as in western arrangements.

The term 'Ikebana' is used of all Japanese floral designs and 'Ikebana International' has been spread throughout the world by the formation of chapters. In England the London Chapter is the official organ for contact with Japan, and by the end of 1970 eight other chapters had been formed. There are many study groups all over the country and a teachers' association which supervises the teaching of Ikebana and tries to ensure that only fully qualified teachers take classes. A training is given which may take as long as five years, and prospective teachers who qualify are awarded diplomas. Thus, high standards of teaching and practice are maintained.

One of the important things to remember in Ikebana is to use the plant material appropriate to the season of the year, tall in winter and early spring, reducing its height it the summer, increasing it again at the approach of autumn.

A delightful type of design known as a landscape or scenic arrangement has the principal aim of representing a natural landscape within a bowl. Careful selection of material can produce a distant or close view of, perhaps, a waterside or hilly scene.

There is an emphasis on colour in all the styles, traditional or modern, and the plant materials are chosen to create pleasing colour effects.

Only after years of study may the student discard the conventional rules and restrictions to give free expression to an arrangement, only then may strange and natural materials be used together without regard for the manner in which they are grown. This should never be attempted by the inexperienced student.

There are two trends in this type of design: one where an imaginary scene arouses emotion by a remembered view and the other where flowers are massed to produce interesting effects of texture, colour and composition.

The equipment needed to produce a good arrangement includes scissors, containers, bases and kenzans. All arrangements in a low or flat container come under the heading 'Moribana', while those arranged in tall or upright containers are 'Nageire'. These latter arrangements are often referred to as the 'throw-in' style and, although they look so easy when demonstrated by an experienced teacher, the beginner will soon find how difficult they are to execute; and a well-trained and qualified teacher is essential. With practice, confidence will be gained so that each placement will be correct and show the character of the exhibitor.

In conclusion: remember that the spiritual feeling which is aroused in the viewer is the most important factor. Restraint and humility can be learned through Ikebana and it becomes both a satisfying medium and an inspiration.

The following photographs are examples:
  20, 53, 54, 103–106

ABSTRACT

Jean Taylor

The arts are so interrelated that movements and interests in one art strongly influence work in other arts. For more than fifty years artists have been painting in the abstract style and it is the style most representative of the twentieth century. It was inevitable that in these days of fast communications the abstract influence would be felt in all the art world including the field of flower arrangement.

Here, however, resistance to abstract trends has been strong – probably because they are in such great contrast to traditional flower arrangements. They have excited considerable controversy and many people have found them difficult to understand. However, few will disagree that abstract styles suit modern buildings and present-day styles in décor. They look well in modern homes and offices, schools and airports although they look very out of place in the traditional homes – for which they are not intended.

Apart from its use in modern settings, many flower arrangers enjoy the mental exercise and challenge of making an abstract design as a work of art on its own and an enjoyable exercise in creativity.

What characterizes abstract design and makes it differ from other designs? Chiefly its lack of realism or naturalism. Some abstracts may be inspired by Nature but they are not in any way naturalistic. This is, of course, what makes them difficult to understand. The dictionary definition of the verb 'to abstract' with reference to art, is 'to present or characterize non-representational designs depicting no recognizable thing, only geometric figures or amorphous creations'. An abstract is a condensed, refined design which concentrates in itself only the essential qualities. That is, it represents the essence and eliminates all unnecessary detail. In painting this is relatively easy as a 'pattern' can be made of lines and squares with an interesting colour scheme, for example by applying paint with a brush on paper or canvas, it may appear unlike anything seen in the world around us. In assembling plant material in an abstract style, the flower arranger faces two major problems. The first is that plant material cannot be altered or manipulated with the same ease and at the will of the designer. Clay, paint, needlework thread and so on can be manipulated much more easily than flowers and foliage which have a delicate, transient beauty very easily damaged. Altering fresh plant material so that it does not appear naturalistic is often most difficult and has led to a tendency to design abstracts using a maximum of dried plant material and driftwood. This is strong and longlasting and can be painted and altered more easily than fresh plant material. Another difficulty concerns the mechanics – the means of holding the plant material in position. Wire and pinholders are not usually attractive and need hiding, and this is often difficult in the simplified, uncluttered abstract designs. This is another reason for the tendency to use dried materials – no device or receptacle is needed for water and the mechanics can be smaller and well hidden.

What makes a flower arrangement into an abstract design? All flower arrangements are abstract in the sense that the plant material is removed from its natural environment – extracted or abstracted from it so that when arranged in a container it does not look as natural as when growing out of doors. But the farther the design departs from using plant material in a naturalistic manner the more abstract is the design. At one end of the scale is the landscape design which is a miniature scene and an exact representation of nature (such as a woodland scene). This cannot be called abstract. At the other end of the imaginary scale is the design which looks completely un-natural – this is a pure abstract. In between are semi-abstracts, using the term in its broadest sense. However the term 'abstract style' is usually reserved for the most unnaturalistic designs – those which do not look at all natural.

In flower arrangement, as in painting, two distinct styles have developed. They differ from each other in that one has subject-matter and the other has not. They are similar in that they eliminate detail and are not realistic.

1. *Non-objective abstract (decorative)*

In this style the plant material is used only for its design qualities – texture, colour, line and form. The sense of design is very strong but no subject-matter is involved. Nothing is either interpreted or intended but a clear de-sign, which stands alone, unrelated in colour and style to anything except perhaps to its setting. In this objective style a yellow chrysanthemum, for example, is not re-garded as an autumn flower but as a yellow sphere with a rough texture; and a bulrush not as a water plant but as a straight line. In the best abstracts there is a strong sense of pattern and simplification, with perfect balance. Inter-est is equated throughout the design and not concentrated in a 'centre of interest' as in traditional design. Several 'emphasis points' carry the eyes around the whole design and there is often no central radiation point. The mechanics are not easy and the arranger needs to be skilful in the use of holding devices before embarking on abstract designs. Matisse said with reference to this style:

'What I dream of is an art of balance, of purity and serenity devoid of troubling or depressing subject matter.'

2. *Objective abstract (interpretative or expressive)*

This style is more compositional and expresses a subject. It has developed from the traditional interpretative styles but does not represent the realistic appearance of the subject-matter. It departs from the literal presentation and instead represents the inner meaning of a subject as it is seen by the particular designer. It is 'insight' not the outward look. It may also interpret the atmosphere or feeling given by a subject or its essence. In any case the statement is simplified in order to strengthen the idea shown. For example, the subject 'childhood' might be represented in the traditional manner by a figurine of a child surrounded by flowers. In objective abstract one designer might represent a boring childhood with young, grey foliage; another, in all black, could show hardship and misery; and yet another a happy childhood of sweetness and simplicity with small daisies and fresh colours. Realistic accessories are not normally used, as in the traditional interpretative designs. However, both abstract styles may use materials other than plant material (for example, copper wire) to give a certain effect in the design. Most flower arrangers feel that in either style plant material should predominate.

Although many people find the abstract designs in flower arrangement difficult to understand, particularly those who love flowers as they appear naturally, the younger generation appreciates these new styles. Due to the present-day art education they have a strongly developed sense of design and find abstract styles stimulating and challenging; they are essentially in sympathy with the newer trends in decor and architecture and in keeping with abstract paintings and sculpture. Many people have come to understand and to like them through a general study of abstract art in which the essential characteristics can be recognized and which gives a new appreciation.

Flower arrangers are always ready to accept a new challenge, however difficult, and to try new fields and consequently abstracts are appearing in greater numbers. Certainly they make the flower arranger feel that she is part of a world movement in art and that she has more freedom to design, without restriction or conformance to custom, than ever before.

The following photographs are examples:
52, 105, 119–123

5 . *ILLUSTRATIONS OF FLOWER ARRANGEMENTS*

In the main these follow the seasons of the year and include examples of the flower arrangements mentioned in the text. The names of the arrangers are given.

Descriptions of the arrangements follow this illustrated section and include the names of the photographers, other than Phyllis Page.

1. **Elegance** *Mary Pope*

2. **Prelude to Spring** *George Foss*

3. **Spring** *Sheila Macqueen*

4. **Western Style** *Dorothy Finlay*

The Hogarth Curve   *Beryl Jackman*   6. **Simple Frontal**

7. **The Crescent**

8. **Invitation to the Ball** (1)
Catherine Hastings

9. **Invitation to the Ball** (2)
Stella Goodman

10. **Quiet Corner** *Doris Starling*

11. **Summer Opulence** *Amy Strachan* and *Freda Eburne*

12. **Hallowe'en** *Peggy Lovell*

13. **Jason with the Golden Fleece** *Joyce Rush*

14. **Blitz** *Ronald Langridge*

15. **Lucrezia Borgia** *Elsie Walker-Jones*

16. **Lace** *Hilda Boyland*

17. **Cotton** *Elizabeth Causton*

18. **Hessian** *Phyllis Allpass*

19. **Brocade** *Joan Edwards*

20. **Fire** *Violet Lawrence*

21. **Pastimes Old and New** *May McDonald*

22. **Summer Wedding** *Mary Lyons*

23. **February Wedding** *Elsie Lamb*

24. **The Altar** *Sally Ades*

25. **In Redenhall Church** *Jocelyn Steward*

26. **The Screen** *Mary Barnard, Mary Biddulph, Pamela Cutler, Iola Rochfort Rae*

The Parish Church of St John the Baptist, Cirencester, Glos.

27. **The Catherine Chapel** *Margaret Peachey*

28. **O'er Hill and Dale** *Patricia Mann*

29. **Liebestraum** *Doris Hickson*

30. **Antiquity** *Peggy Lovell*

31. **From a French Garden** *Colette Baumann*

Fragrance *Eileen Marsh*

33. **Down the Garden Path** *Ivy Joynes*

34. **In a Basket** *Peggy Lovell*

35. **Horn of Plenty** *Elsie Lamb*

36. *Bess Woods*   **In a Cornucopia**   37. *Helen Fenwick*

38. **The Buffet Table** *Howard Plank*

39. **Viewed from all Sides** *Ruth Jackson*

40. *Margaret Young*   **Jack-in-a-Box**   41. *Peggy Lovell*

42. *Doris Hopkins* **Hats Off!** 43. *Margaret Wilbond*

44. **In Claverton Manor** (1)
Joyce Henry

45. **In Claverton Manor** (2)
Rosemary Laidlau

46. **Ascension**
Frances Matthews

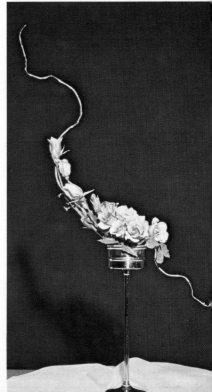

47. **With a Delicate Air**
Anita Rollins

48. *Linda Croucher*

49. *Edith Wise*

In Glass Container

50. *George Smith*

51. *Sylvia Pullan*

52. **Sorrow** *Jean Taylor*

53. **An Element** *Edna Blumson*

54. **Simplicity** *Charlotte Wright*

The Delphinium Society *Howard Plank*

7. **The Daffodil Society** *Charlotte Wright*

56. **The Rose Society** *George Foss*

58. **The Iris Society** *Anne Tomalin*

59. **In the Geffrye Museum** *Elsie Lamb*

60. **Dutch Period** *Betty Tindall*

61. **Delft Pottery** *Betty Tindall*

62. **Victorian Posy** *Mary Pope*

63. **The Old Master** *Douglas Hurst*

64. **Polyanthus**   *Mabel Johnson*   65. **Study in Yellow**

66. **Australiana**
Estelle Normand

67. **In the Modern Style**
Beth Higgs

68. **Spring Sentry** *Frances Matthews*

69. **Beauty in Simplicity** *Iona Trevor Jones*

70. **Waratahs**
Thelma Arlom

71. **Celosia**
Thelma Arlom

72. **Autumn** *Adèle Gotobed*

73. **From an Autumn Garden** *Adèle Gotobed*

74. **Geraniums**   *Louisa Scott*   75. **Simplicity**

76. **Little Poppet** *Kit Gasser*

For the Dolls' House *Rosamond Fuller*

77. **Time Stands Still** *Kit Gasser*

79. **Silver Gem** *Rosamond Fuller*

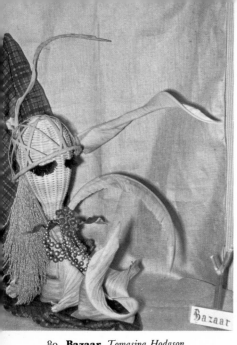

80. **Bazaar** *Tomasina Hodgson*

81. **The Blue Dragon** *Jean McKreel Cla*

82. **The Chelsea Pensioner** **In the Kings Road, Chelsea** 83. **Chelsea Art Students**
   Elizabeth Churchill   *Beryl Ivory*

84. **Foliage** *Dorothy Tuffin*

85. **The Museum Piece** *Evelyn Galley*

86. **In Claverton Manor**
    Winifred Simpson

87. **Ming** *Katharine Hare*

88. **London Museums**
    Gwendolen Yates

89. **Green Grow the Rushes O!**
Marjory Wright

90. **The Water Garden**
Sybil Emberton

91. **Green Jade** *Gay Curme*

92. **Summer in Winter** *Sylvia Pullan*

93. **Winter Picture**
Doris Hickson

94. **Lasting Beauty**
Doris Hickson

95. **The Unusual** *Jean Louwrens*

96. **The Calabash** *Kitty Kimber*

Papyrus and Bixa Pods *Henny Dickenson*

98. **From Overseas** *Wilfred Kenyon*

99. **The Shell**

100. **Wall Hanging**   *Sylvia Pullan*   101. **On a Raffia Mat**

102. **Amber** *Iona Trevor Jones*

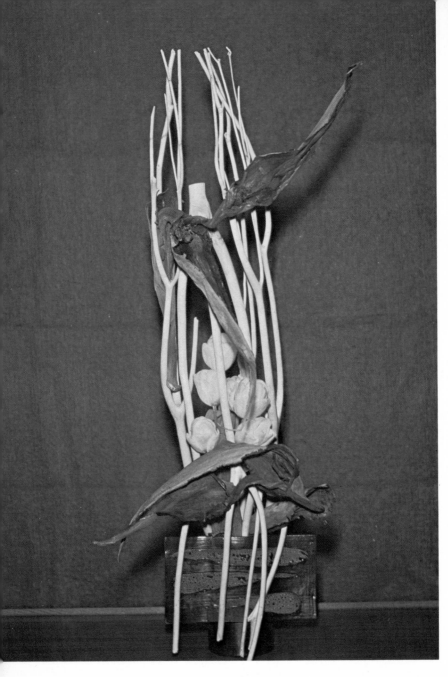

103. **Captive** *Stella Coe*

104. **Tranquillity** *Stella Coe*

105. **Windswept** *Maud Cole*

106. **Cherry Blossom** *Maud Cole*

107. **Cyprus Green** *Ida Ingle*

108. **Holy Night** *Marian Aaronson*

109. **The Nativity** *Mary Lee*

110. **Purity** *Margaret Couper*

111. **Pickwickian Christmas**
Blanche Bedford

112. **Edwardian Elegance**
Jean Taylor

113. **The Sparkle of Christmas**
Members of the London and Overseas Association

114. **Christmas Gift** *Jean Taylor*

115. **For a London Flat** *Mary Lee*

116. **For the Drawing Room** *Edith W*

117. **Pot-et-Fleur** *Violet Stevenson*

118. **For the Town House** *Edith Wi*

119. **Blue and Gold** *Marian Aaronson*

120. **Kenyan Treasures** *Marian Aaronson*

Thorn Construction *Marian Aaronson*

122. **Metallic Splendour** *Marian Aaronson*

123. **Play on a Circle** *Jean Taylor*

6. DESCRIPTIONS OF ILLUSTRATIONS

1 Elegance Mary Pope *Dorchester, Dorset.*

The berberis and the delicate colouring of the *Epimedium* leaves enhance the subtle colouring of the cymbidium orchids, so cleverly arranged in the Regency ormolu jug.

2 Prelude to Spring George Foss, *Petersham, Surrey.*

This simple arrangement (an asymmetrical triangle), which would bring a thought of spring to any room, consists of hardy outdoor foliage and flowers: alder, golden euonymus, bergenia, *Helleborus foetidus*, ivy and heather, with the addition of *Billbergia windii* and guelder rose (*Viburnum opulus*). The interesting base is carved from a tree root.

3 Spring Sheila Macqueen, *Leverstock Green, Herts.*

This elegant triangular arrangement of outstanding beauty is composed of daphne, pink hyacinths, 'Delightful' tulips, *Helleborus orientalis* and *H. foetidus* with grey eucalyptus and *Begonia rex* leaves.

4 Western Style Dorothy Finlay, *Ferny Creek, Victoria, Australia.*

Flowering branches of *Parrotia persica*, *Protea neriifolia*, red flax and *Epimedium* foliage, all from the garden of the arranger, make this elegant arrangement.

It is an example of an asymmetrical triangle. *Photo: A. Gulliver.*

5 The Hogarth Curve Beryl Jackman *Hascombe, Surrey.*

The same plant material as in 'The Crescent' (below) has been used for this Hogarth curve. It is arranged in a candle-cup on top of a brass candle-stick.

6 Simple Frontal Beryl Jackman

Pussy willow forms the outline of this simple frontal arrangement in a shallow dish. *Mahonia japonica* and bergenia leaves make the background for the tulips and daffodils.

7 The Crescent Beryl Jackman

Broom, which has been 'stroked' into curves for the outline with cupressus and wild arum leaves, shows up the daffodils and tulips which follow the shape of the crescent.

8 'Invitation to the Ball' (1) Catherine Hastings, *St Albans, Herts.*

A simple arrangement of freesias, pale pink carnations and lime-green hydrangeas with the foliage of *Senecio laxifolius* and *Cineraria maritima* in a pale blue Chinese vase. The flowers portray the delicate colouring of the pink and mauve embroidery on the Chinese fan.

9 'Invitation to the Ball' (2) Stella Goodman, *Luton, Beds.*

Ophelia roses, carnations and greyish green *Begonia rex* leaves, with shiny black privet berries recessed in the centre, are arranged in a wrought-iron container. The curved broom outline and the black lace fan give the impression of the dance, while the matt pink silk background with pink and grey net represents the gown.

10 Quiet Corner Doris Starling, *Chigwell, Essex.*

A non-competitive exhibit staged at a Floral Luncheon held at the Savoy Hotel in aid of The Forces Help Society and Lord Roberts Workshops.

The gentle solomon's seal harmonizes with the elegance of the bird; the white lily-flowered tulips pick up the white in the container, the rocks and the flowers of the solomon's seal. The bird is a transition from white to black, bringing unity between the black lining of the dish and stand.

11 Summer Opulence Amy Strachan, *Thames Ditton*, and Freda Eburne, *Surbiton, Surrey.*

An elegant arrangement of delphiniums, paeonies, foxgloves, astilbe, roses, *Lilium regale*, clematis and sweet peas is staged with green and white funkia leaves, in a Dresden china figure container against a soft pale green drape. The fruits show up well on the deep green velvet base. It won a prize for Surrey Floral Decoration Society in London.

12 Hallowe'en Peggy Lovell, *Walton-on-Thames, Surrey.*

Twists of chestnut bark, broom, glycerined aspidistra leaves, *Kniphofia*, dahlias and virginia creeper leaves were used. The container is an inverted china lampshade painted black with a stiff rim to represent a witch's hat. The cat and witch's broom complete the picture.

13 Jason with the Golden Fleece Joyce Rush, *Rayleigh, Essex.*

This is a clever arrangement, depicting Jason holding aloft the Golden Fleece. The texture and the colour of the mimosa, forsythia, tulips and freesia, together with the shape of the arrangement, given the appearance of a golden fleece. The pieces of pine bark at the base of the figure simulate the rocks.

14 Blitz Ronald Langridge, *Hassocks, Sussex.*

This is a dramatic arrangement. The effect of fire is produced with purple beech, *Rhus cotinus*, 'Baccara' roses, scarlet carnations and gladioli, orange, scarlet and crimson zinnias. Tiger lilies and *Kniphofia* depict the flames. The background is canvas painted with charcoal under a black net. Red and orange net gives the glow of the fire. At the top a Spitfire is seen diving into the flames.

15 Lucrezia Borgia Elsie Walker-Jones, *Slough, Bucks.*

Garden flowers in purple, blue-mauve, pink, puce and red colouring are arranged in a seventeenth-century flagon. Poisonous bryony, hemlock and deadly nightshade, together with the bee, show the 'sting' in the cup.

16 Lace Hilda Boyland, *Hinchley Wood, Surrey.*

This delicate arrangement of gypsophila, white catananche and white delphiniums is a clever interpretation of 'Lace'.

17 Cotton Elizabeth Causton, *Cobham, Surrey.*

The poppies, cornflowers and yellow and white daisies are arranged in a white urn to repeat the design of cotton material.

18 Hessian Phyllis Allpass, *Tyrrells Wood, Surrey.*

This striking arrangement of foreign seed-pods is arranged in a rope basket on a piece of hessian. The rough texture of the materials and background suggest the title of the picture.

19 Brocade Joan Edwards, *New Eltham, London.*

The dried paeony seed-pods, poppy, antirrhinum and nigella seed-heads, hydrangea flower-heads, aspidistra, *Grevillea*, berberis and magnolia leaves and dried ivy have been painted and sprayed to match the brocade background to perfection.

20 Fire Violet Lawrence, *London.*

This modern design of dyed red grass, scarlet bulrushes, scarlet tulips and thorn twig was an exhibit at a Home Counties Area Spring show at Southend.

21 Pastimes Old and New May McDonald, *Thames Ditton, Surrey.*

This delightful composition suggests a hobby or occupation. Wild grasses, shepherd's purse, viburnum berries, buds of *helenium*, variegated honeysuckle and ivy, with a drape of soft green linen,

emphasize the texture and delicate colouring of the sampler, which have remained in perfect condition for nearly two hundred years.

22 Summer Wedding Mary Lyons, *Guildford, Surrey.*

This is one of a pair of pedestal arrangements in Christ Church, Guildford, arranged for a July wedding. The white and cream stocks, gladioli and larkspur are all suitable flowers for use in a church.

23 February Wedding Elsie Lamb, *Thames Ditton, Surrey.*

The eucalyptus and camellia foliage with sprays of forsythia show to advantage the white lilac, white American spray chrysanthemums and yellow and white gladioli. *Lilium longiflorum* form the centre and white carnations flow over the front. They are arranged on a 3-ft wrought-iron pedestal, painted to tone with the flowers. It was one of a pair at the chancel steps of the thirteenth-century church of St Nicholas, Thames Ditton, Surrey. The yellow flowers give warmth to the arrangement designed for a February wedding.

24 The Altar Sally Ades, *Oxshott, Surrey.*

Lilium longiflorum in an elegant brass vase are the flowers used on the altar of St Andrew's Church, Oxshott, Surrey. Their simplicity gives beauty to the Cross and the arrangement of the lilies leads the eyes upwards.

25 In Redenhall Church Jocelyn Steward, *Tunstead, Norfolk.*

This bold green and cream pedestal arrangement of unsophisticated plant material from the garden shows well against the wooden panelling. The golden privet and *Weigela florida variegata*, with the bold leaves of *Sambucus aurea*, provide a background for the striking seed-heads of the giant angelica and stems of *Euphorbia robbiae*. The dainty *Aruncus sylvester* and *Alstroemeria aurantiaca* add the highlights to the mass of foliage.

26 The Screen of St John the Baptist Church, *Cirencester, Glos.*: Mary Barnard, Mary Biddulph, Pamela Cutler, Iola Rochfort Rae.

The screen is decorated with flowers of red and flame colouring, with flame-coloured arrangements at the foot of the choir stalls to lead the eye to the high altar.

27 The Catherine Chapel Margaret Peachey, *Cirencester, Glos.*

This elegant pair of matching pedestals in shades of lime, cream and gold stand each side of the altar. The tall spikes of wild iris and 'Green Woodpecker' gladioli point upwards to the beautiful fan-vaulted roof. Grey cardoon leaves and long, arching sprays of *Stephandra tanacaea* make the background for the *Lilium* 'Golden Regale'.

28 O'er Hill and Dale Patricia Mann, *Aldershot, Hants.*

This picture shows the charm of wild flowers when cleverly arranged. Dock, lady's bedstraw, harebells, creeping bell-flower, bracken, foxglove leaves, whortle-berry and rowan berries, mignonette seed-heads and linaria are used on a natural yew base.

29 Liebestraum Doris Hickson, *Walton-on-Thames, Surrey*

The wild grasses, brown reeds, thistles, wild iris leaves, ferns, foxglove leaves, spurge, wild red poppies and wild oats, give a feeling of drowsy summer, completed by the little dog asleep. This won 1st prize at a Surrey Floral Decoration Society summer show.

30 Antiquity Peggy Lovell, *Walton-on-Thames, Surrey.*

A dead branch, lichen twigs, dried *Stachys lanata*, with dried ferns and wild seed-heads, sea holly and fungi give the cold atmosphere of antiquity. The whole composition is in grey and grey-green colouring. An ancient figurine represents Father Time, whose hair and whiskers are made of old man's beard and whose scythe is a eucalyptus leaf.

31 From a French Garden Colette Baumann, *Paris, France.*

Daisies and delphiniums in a little cart make this delightful arrangement. *Photo: Colette Baumann.*

32 Fragrance Eileen Marsh, *Ashtead, Surrey.*

This charming arrangement is composed of cream stocks and honeysuckle 'Halliana'.

33 Down the Garden Path Ivy Joynes, *Bexley Heath, Kent.*

Cerise paeonies, pink and cerise pyrethrums, pink stocks and the leaves of *Hosta* 'albo picta' are arranged in a garden basket.

34 In a Basket Peggy Lovell, *Walton-on-Thames, Surrey*.

This arrangement in a basket is composed of *Lilium dalhansonii*, green hydrangea heads, *Eriogonum umbellatum*, with ivy, *Epimedium* and virginia creeper leaves, and ferns.

35 Horn of Plenty Elsie Lamb, *Thames Ditton, Surrey*

A wicker cornucopia pours forth a wealth of colourful fruit and foliage. The shiny green camellia leaves act as a foil for the smooth plums, apples and aubergine which contrast with the bloom on the peaches and grapes. Added interest is provided by the shape of the grey stone bottle in the background.

36 In a Cornucopia (1) Bess Woods, *Chalfont St Giles, Bucks*.

This clever arrangement of aquilegia, *Cobaea scandens* and sweet peas, with *Begonia rex* leaves as foliage, was one of a pair staged at an exhibition of flower arrangements in Blenheim Palace, held in aid of the Oxford Committee for Famine Relief.

37 In a Cornucopia (2) Helen Fenwick, *Chalfont St Giles, Bucks* .

This charming arrangement af ranunculus and yellow broom was one of a pair staged in Blenheim Palace at an exhibition of flower arrangements in aid of the Oxford Committee for Famine Relief.

38 The Buffet Table Howard Plank. *Teteko, Bay of Plenty, New Zealand*.

This elegant arrangement for a buffet table was in an exhibition of flower arrangements held at the Manor House,

Godalming. The colour harmony of the 'Super Star' roses, azaleas, 'Harvest Moon' carnations, tellima, hellebore, *Anemone pulsatilla* seed-heads, grass seed-heads and lime-green *Enkianthus* is particularly pleasing with the gilt candlestick and Danish gold candles.

39 Viewed from all Sides Ruth Jackson, *Salfords, Surrey*.

This beautiful arrangement is made in a Portuguese green and white glass fruit bowl which is placed on a base covered with velvet to tone with the red grapes. The flowers include auriculas in several shades from yellow to claret, 'Margaret' and 'Sweet Harmony' Rembrandt tulips, lime-green tobacco plant and *Primula obconica* flower-heads picked after the flowers had fallen. The foliage used is *Berberis atropurpurea*, alchemilla, aquilegia and hart's tongue ferns which were just unfolding; green and red 'Emperor' grapes complete the picture.

40 Jack-in-a-Box (1) Margaret Young, *Penn, Bucks*.

Pelargoniums and 'Garnette' roses make the colour in this gay box which was a prizewinner in the 'Jack-in-a-Box' class at a Royal Windsor Rose and Horticultural Societies' annual Show.

41 Jack-in-the-Box (2) Peggy Lovell, *Walton-on-Thames, Surrey*.

The red berries, lilies of the valley, dark brown wallflowers, *Anemone pulsatilla* seed-heads representing the smoke, and geranium and grey *Senecio* leaves harmonize with the grey and white box, making this prize-winner.

42 Hats Off (1) Doris Hopkins

This gay arrangement won a prize in the novice section for an arrangement in a hat at a Royal Windsor Rose and Horticultural Societies' Show which is held annually in the grounds of Windsor Castle. The cornflowers, geums, marguerites and grey-green foliage are arranged in a straw boater hat which is trimmed with striped ribbon.

43 Hats Off (2) Margaret Wilbond, *Windsor, Berkshire.*

This gay arrangement in a hat was a prize winner in the novice section at a Royal Windsor Rose and Horticultural Societies' Show. A shallow dish was placed in the crown of a child's chip straw hat and filled in profusion with 'Paul Scarlet' roses. The crown of the hat appears to be entirely composed of roses.

44 In Claverton Manor (1) Joyce Henry, *Durban, South Africa.*

These unusual flowers, picked from gardens in Durban, were flown to England by courtesy of B.O.A.C. and were arranged in the hall of Claverton Manor, the American Museum near Bath, for the 'Flowers and Costume' Festival.

Anthuriums, proteas of cream and green colouring, red bixa pods, croton, *Dracaena* and strelitzia leaves were used together with tulips, guelder rose (*Viburnum opulus*) and copper beech from England.

45 In Claverton Manor (2) Rosemary Laidlau, *Umhtazi, Natal, South Africa.*

This charming arrangement was also in the entrance hall to Claverton Manor and the flowers and foliage were flown to England by B.O.A.C. especially for the 'Flowers and Costume' Festival.

The arrangement includes pink and rose varieties of unusual proteas, croton and *Dracaena* foliage, indigenous pods from gardens and farms near Durban, where the 'puff balls' were growing wild. The bronze cones and protea foliage are from The Cape.

46 Ascension Frances Matthews, *Portland, Oregon, U.S.A.*

This outstanding arrangement gained the Supreme Award in the Pacific Region in 1963, judged by the National Council of Garden Clubs. The title 'Ascension' is suggested by the coils on the straw mat through the circular design of the hand-made earthen jug to the ascending section of dried kelp. Three 'Fugi' chrysanthemums and *Antennaria* 'Oat's Ear' foliage complete the design. Space has been used as a positive element instead of the usual interval between solids. *Photo: Delano Photographies, Portland, Oregon, U.S.A.*

47 With a Delicate Air Anita Rollins, *Portland, Oregon, U.S.A.*

This striking arrangement of 'Lu Lu' roses in a glass comport won a Blue Ribbon Award at the Portland Rose Show. The whitened wisteria branch gives shape and movement to the picture. The container was made by Anita Rollins. *Photo: William Vale, Portland, Oregon.*

48 In Glass Container (1) Linda Croucher, *Ashtead, Surrey.*

This unusual arrangement shows an effective use of brightly coloured glass. It was an entry at an Ashtead Autumn

Show, in the class 'Sleek Sophistication'. *Moluccella*, *Cana* and *Begonia rex* leaves were arranged with green *Nicotiana* and green *Amaranthus caudatus*.

49 In Glass Container (2) Edith Wise, *Chelsea, London.*

The sprays of *Mahonia japonica*, variegated holly and holly berries make a striking arrangement in the tall glass. It won a prize at a London and Overseas Autumn Show.

50 In Glass Container (3) George Smith, *Halifax, W. Yorkshire.*

A modern glass bottle of vertical line stimulates the feeling of ascending rhythm in a group of dried material typified by the swerve of glycerined aspidistra leading to the upward movement of wood roses, brown desert spoons and iris seed-pods. The circular mat of natural raffia improves the balance and forms a link between the arrangement and its surroundings.

51 In Glass Container (4) Sylvia Pullan, *Brockley, Nr. Bristol, Avon.*

Only a close look will reveal that these flowers have been preserved. The gay zinnias show up well against the *Senecio* leaves and the dainty pink and blue annual larkspurs add charm to the arrangement in a tall blue glass goblet.

52 Sorrow Jean Taylor, *Knutsford, Cheshire.*

An example of an objective abstract arrangement. The arum lily, blackthorn branches and the dried strelitzia leaf are placed in a modern container on a Honister base. *Photo: D. Rendell.*

53 An Element Edna Blumson, *Brookman's Park, Herts.*

The two *Clivia* flowers have been cleverly placed with dried mauve seaweed, a piece of stripped tree ivy and two ivy leaves.

54 Simplicity Charlotte Wright, *Belfast.*

The twisted wisteria branch adds movement and interest to the two arum lilies. Rhododendron foliage gives weight at the base.

55 The Delphinium Society Howard Plank, *Teteko, Bay of Plenty, New Zealand.*

Dark and pale mauve and cream delphiniums are used, interspersed with feathery cream *Thalictrum* and *Calocephalus brownii*, with large *Begonia rex* leaves to give the necessary weight at the base, make this mass arrangement which won a prize in the 'Specialist Society' class at the National Competitions, London.

56 The Rose Society George Foss, *Petersham, Surrey.*

This elegant arrangement of 'Carol' roses in the delicate porcelain container would add charm to any room.

57 The Daffodil Society Charlotte Wright, *Belfast, N. Ireland.*

This simple arrangement of daffodils with alder gives the feeling of spring.

58 The Iris Society Anne Tomalin, *Fleet, Hants.*

This arrangement is composed of *Iris spuria*, ferns, hosta, *Cardiocrinum giganteum* leaves and driftwood. It won a prize in the 'Specialist Society' class at the National Competitions in London.

59 In the Geffrye Museum Elsie Lamb, *Thames Ditton, Surrey.*

This delicate arrangement, in the Regency Room at the Geffrye Museum, Shoreditch, of pale blue delphiniums, nigella, paeonies, roses, artemisia, arum lilies, bergamot, pinks, foxgloves, campanulas and antirrhinums is on a torchere by a window.

60 Dutch Period Betty Tindall, *Dorchester, Dorset.*

This seventeenth-century Dutch period arrangement is in a black pottery container and comprises carnations, tulips, polyanthus, narcissi, iris, roses and viburnum: all flowers used by the Dutch painters of the period.

61 Delft Pottery Betty Tindall, *Dorchester, Dorset.*

This arrangement of tulips, anemones, narcissi and irises in a Delft vase is a colourful example of the seventeenth-century Dutch style, 'Still Life' paintings.

62 Victorian Posy Mary Pope, *Dorchester, Dorset.*

Polyanthus, wallflowers, double daisies, pelargoniums, bridal wreath, heuchera, white bells, yellow archangel, spurge and maidenhair fern have been woven cleverly together to make this charming arrangement in a Victorian china vase, typical of that period.

63 The Old Master Douglas Hurst, *Surbiton, Surrey.*

An impression of Dutch flower painting in the seventeenth to eighteenth centuries. The flowers used include tulips, lilac, *Clivia*, hyacinths, foxgloves, stocks, polyanthus, carnations, iris, crown imperials, white jasmine and *Anemone pulsatilla*. A bird's nest and grapes were frequently used in these period flower pictures.

64 Polyanthus Mabel Johnson, *Belfast, N. Ireland.*

This natural arrangement of polyanthus in an interesting piece of driftwood decorates an old wooden chest.

65 Study in Yellow Mabel Johnson, *Belfast, N. Ireland.*

Yellow tulips and freesias backed with begonia leaves, make this charming arrangement on a pewter breadboard. The driftwood gives movement to the arrangement.

66 Australiana Estelle Normand, *Melbourne, Victoria, Australia.*

This dried Ikebana arrangement is in the style of the Sogetsu School and has been made with two tall stems of the native blackboys, white leaf-bases of the leaves of blackgins, a fan of immature leaves and a cross-section from the trunk of a blackboy surrounded by orange veritcordia. Sweetcorn leaves fill in the base. *Photo: Arthur Gulliver.*

67 In the Modern Style Beth Higgs, *Melbourne, Victoria, Australia.*

Seed-heads of agapanthus with naturally bent stems, native Australian cycad palm leaves and white carnations are placed in a modern orange-coloured container. *Photo: Arthur Gulliver.*

68 Spring Sentry Frances Matthews, *Portland, Oregon, U.S.A.*

Camellia sasanqua 'Apple Blossom' is arranged with the foliage of *Iris spuria* on a slab of black stone. The two 'marsh birds', sculptured by the weather, were found on the Oregon sand dunes. Moss and smooth stones complete the picture, giving balance and the illusion of water. *Photo: Delano Photographies, Portland, Oregon.*

69 Beauty in Simplicity Iona Trevor Jones, *Pontfadog, Clwyd, North Wales.*

This arrangement is a good example of what can be achieved with a minimum of flowers and foliage when skilfully placed. The twisted ivy branches and two white 'Mount Tacona' tulips are secured on a pinholder. This is concealed with pieces of green glass rock which matches the colours of the deep green glass bowl.

70 Waratahs Thelma Arlom, *Roseville, New South Wales, Australia.*

This striking arrangement in a brown ceramic bowl of waratahs and *Telopea speciosissima* is framed by a polished wood root from a river bank. *Photo: John Arlom.*

71 Celosia Thelma Arlom, *Roseville, New South Wales, Australia*

This unusual arrangement is composed of driftwood and *Celosia*. *Photo: John Arlom.*

72 Autumn Adele Gotobed, *Hounslow, Middlesex.*

This triangular arrangement in a large copper urn shows the glorious colouring of autumn. *Berberis thunbergii, B. atropurpurea, Callicarpa* berries, *Hosta,* paeony and purple vine leaves make a colourful background for the dahlias, chrysanthemums and red geraniums. The New Zealand flax gives height to the arrangement.

73 From an Autumn Garden Adele Gotobed, *Hounslow, Middlesex.*

This charming collection of flowers, foliage and berries was gathered from a garden near London at the end of October and arranged in an old tea caddy.

Berberis, Callicarpa berries, *Echeveria,* vine leaves and the seed-heads of the staghorn sumac show to advantage the roses and make an interesting mixed design.

74 Geraniums Louisa Scott, *Gore, Southland, New Zealand.*

This charming arrangement in a frosted glass vase shows what can be achieved with the use of only one type of flower. *Photo: E. L. Scott.*

75 Simplicity Louisa Scott, *Gore, Southland, New Zealand.*

The charm of this arrangement lies in its simplicity. An apple twig, three sprays of ivy and three golden yarra heads have been used to great effect. *Photo: E. L. Scott.*

76 Little Poppet Kit Gasser, *Walton-on-Thames, Surrey.*

This tiny arrangement in a poppy seed-head is perfect for a pixie's tea-party. The tiny flowers include daisies, roses, statice and white heather. All these have been preserved carefully in borax.

77 Time Stands Still Kit Gasser, *Walton-on-Thames, Surrey.*

The beauty of the little roses will remain for a very long time as they have been preserved in borax and have retained the soft pink colouring. Golden heather, box leaves and alder seed-cones complete this little arrangement in a man's pocket watch.

78 For the Doll's House Rosamond Fuller, *Epsom, Surrey.*

Broom 'Praecox', saxifraga, berberis, hyssop and tiny fern fronds are fixed in Oasis to make this charming little arrangement on a minute brass tray.

79 Silver Gem Rosamond Fuller, *Epsom, Surrey.*

The tiny flowers, arranged in a silver box, are *Spiraea thunbergii*, forget-me-nots and miniature geraniums. The foliage consists of small leaves of pelargonium 'Silver Gem' and tiny pieces of sedum.

80 Bazaar Tomasina Hodgson, *Esher, Surrey.*

This striking arrangement illustrates the 'Beat' fashion boutique 'Bazaar' in the King's Road, Chelsea.

The design is achieved with twisted dried banana leaves, date palm, artichoke heads, bean pods, tropical nuts and beads, all woven round a cane display head with black raffia eyelashes and a Chinese basket hat. The natural salt-fired pottery container was made by the exhibitor. This won an award in 'The

King's Road, Chelsea' class at an Exhibition in the Chenil Galleries, London. Nos. 94–96 also won awards.

81 The Blue Dragon Jean McKreel Clarke, *Stanford-le-Hope, Essex.*

This represents the many antique shops to be found in the King's Road, Chelsea.

The Chinese virburnum and beech branches, covered with lichen, are arranged in an authentic antique Japanese bronze container. The blue and white begging rice bowls, the pilgrims' platter and the antique tree, with leaves of jade and flowers of lapis lazuli, complete the picture.

82 The Chelsea Pensioner Elizabeth Churchill, *Burgess Hill, Sussex.*

The red tunics worn by the Chelsea Pensioners, so often seen in the King's Road, are depicted by the scarlet flowers, while the medals, 'Sam Brown' and khaki trousers complete the picture.

83 Chelsea Art Students Beryl Ivory, *Southwick, Sussex.*

The arum leaves represent the artist's palette and the pink daffodils and orange parrot tulips the colours in the palette, and the bulrushes are the brushes. The arrangement is placed on old corduroy trousers representing the Chelsea Art Students. The picture of Nell Gwynne was painted by Beryl Ivory.

84 Foliage Dorothy Tuffin, *Cuckfield, Sussex.*

Dried wild foxglove seed-heads and Spanish chestnut leaves, which have been glycerined, make this unusual arrangement. At the back is a 'Monkey Pod' from Singapore. The green of the bergenia and rhododendron leaves shows off the walnut base. The carved mountain goat completes the picture.

85 The Museum Piece Evelyn Galley, *Wanstead, London.*

The arrangement of exotic seed-heads with leaves of aspidistra, laurel, magnolia, berberis and mahonia is massed around a fossilized vertebra of *Bos primigenus*, aurochs or giant ox, with a piece of driftwood to represent the head of an animal. This fossil was found at Ilford, Essex.

86 In Claverton Manor Winifred Simpson, *Stoke Poges, Bucks.*

This dried arrangement composed of bulrushes, dried fern, magnolia leaves, lotus pods, cones, allium heads, poppy heads, thistles and dried gladioli spikes was an exhibit in Claverton Manor, near Bath.

87 Ming Katharine Hare, *Hove, Sussex.*

Dried palm leaves and glycerined laurel leaves with magnolia and iris seed-pods and a piece of fungus surround the Ming figure which is placed on a warm brown base.

88 London Museums Gwendolen Yates, *Leicester.*

The centre of interest in this arrangement is the three cardoons. Also used in the arrangement are tulip seed-heads, *Iris foetidissima*, old man's beard, begonia leaves and skeleton magnolia leaves. Driftwood, a piece of bleached ivy and white fungus give the feeling of age to the arrangement.

89 Green Grow the Rushes O! Marjory Wright, *Felpham, Sussex.*

This water scene is arranged in a stone bowl with a pale blue lining. The leaves and seed-heads of *Iris sibirica*, various rushes, leaves of hosta, *Primula florindae* and moss give the feeling of the lakeside. The bird which is carved from an Indian bone completes the picture.

90 The Water Garden Sybil Emberton, *Hindhead, Surrey.*

Grasses (*Elymus glaucus*), fruits of a wild pondweed, foliage of *Cynara cardunculus* and a porcelain heron on a pewter dish cleverly portray the peace of a water garden.

91 Green Jade Gay Curme, *Worplesdon, Surrey.*

This clever arrangement to depict 'Green Jade' is composed of wild iris and artichoke leaves, lamb's ear, equisetum and *Echeveria*. The antique Chinese plate on which the arrangement is made is over one hundred and fifty years old. The background of bamboo matting makes a perfect setting for 'Green Jade'.

92 Summer in Winter Sylvia Pullan, *Brockley, Avon.*

This colourful arrangement of dried flowers shows the progress that has been made in preserving summer flowers for use in the winter months. The gay African marigolds show well against the dried magnolia and rhododendron leaves. The stripped branches of ivy give movement and complete the design.

93 Winter Picture Doris Hickson, *Walton-on-Thames, Surrey.*

A formal design of preserved and dried flowers makes this attractive picture in an old gilt frame. The tussore silk background enhances the colour of the leek seed-heads, hydrangea florets, helechrysums, sprays of erica, larkspur, delphinium and statice.

94 Lasting Beauty Doris Hickson, *Walton-on-Thames, Surrey.*

A painted grey frame with a pale grey velvet background is the setting for this picture. Dried grasses, corn, poppy seedheads, nicandra, *Moluccella*, helichrysums, hydrangea florets and two large black-eyed susans are used to great effect with carrot flowers, ferns and leaves to complete the picture. All the flowers and leaves have been carefully preserved and will retain their colour for a long time.

95 The Unusual Jean Louwrens, *Salisbury, Rhodesia.*

This unusual arrangement, on a round hand-made mat, is composed of pherocarpus, angoliensis, leucaena, abizzia, hyphaens – palm and wild cones.

It was flown to London for the National Competitions from Salisbury, Rhodesia, with Nos. 96, 97 and 98.

96 The Calabash Kitty Kimber, *Bulawayo, Rhodesia.*

Mimosa seed-pods are fashioned into flowers and are arranged in a calabash with aloe and preserved fiddlewood leaves.

97 Papyrus and Bixa Pods Henny Dickenson, *Salisbury, Rhodesia.*

Papyrus and bixa pods make this gay arrangement of unusual material.

98 From Overseas Wilfred Kenyon, *Salisbury, Rhodesia.*

Banana calices, sterculia, jacaranda pods, *Tamarindus indica*, canavalia, jack beans and asclepias are cleverly arranged on a bamboo base.

99 The Shell Sylvia Pullan, *Brockley, Avon.*

The delicate colours of the Christmas and lenten roses and the leaves of amelanchier are reflected in the edges of the shell. It is hard to believe that these are preserved and not fresh from the garden.

100 Wall Hanging Sylvia Pullan, *Brockley, Somerset.*

This interesting collection of dried montbretia, plantian, catalpa, (India bean), rue, love-in-a-mist, rhododendron, iris, poppy, beech, figwort, paeony, eucalyptus, shoe-fly, honesty and catananche is cleverly arranged with pieces of dried bracken and glycerined beech leaves on to a straw mat to make a charming wall hanging.

101 On a Raffia Mat Sylvia Pullan, *Brockley, Avon.*

The leaves used in this colourful arrangement have been pressed under a carpet between newspaper and stuck on a raffia mat with a strong adhesive. The grey leaves are *Senecio*, grevillia and alchemilla; the green ivy and fern; the red eucalyptus, maple and aronia. The red-green is amelanchier and the underside of fern leaves, showing the sporengia, gives the brown colouring.

102 Amber Iona Trevor Jones, *Pontfadog, Clwyd, North Wales.*

Arum lilies, lotus seed-heads, brown bulrushes, desert spoons, amber-coloured alabaster grapes, with the young foliage of the wild sycamore, make this outstanding 'Amber' arrangement.

103 Captive Stella Coe, *The London Chapter of Ikebana International.*

This dramatic arrangement in a modern container of bleached branches, dried strelitzia and white tulips is in the Japanese abstract style.

104 Tranquillity Stella Coe, *The London Chapter of Ikebana International.*

Arum lilies with tree ivy and a piece of root in a flat 'moribana' container make this tranquil arrangement in the Japanese traditional style.

105 Windswept Maud Cole, *Kenton, Middlesex.*

This Japanese arrangement, full of movement, decorated the Elizabethan home of Mr and Mrs Noel-Dore at an exhibition staged by members of the Home Counties Area.

106 Cherry Blossom Maud Cole, *Kenton, Middlesex.*

This is a clever arrangement seen at an Open Exhibition of the London Chapter of Ikebana International to illustrate

the poem by Issa – 'In my life as in the twilight a bell sounds, I enjoy the freshness of Spring'.

Cherry blossom, erica and azalea leaves are arranged in an ancient Japanese vase. An ancient bell completes the picture.

107 Cyprus Green Ida Ingle, *Zululand, South Africa.*

The beauty of the Cypru green ceramic jar, made by the arranger, is enhanced by the dried arrangement which encircles it. The curving lines of the dried broom are strengthened with glycerine-preserved eucalyptus while the dried pink bracts and flowers of bougainvillea 'Natalia' and the ball-like clusters of brunia give the subtle colouring.

The green glass of a ship's porthole is used for the base. *Photo: David Leeney.*

108 Holy Night Marian Aaronson *Upper Wanborough, Wiltshire.*

The white bleached branch repeats the gentle curve of the Virgin Mary as she kneels in prayer. The black background intensifies the 'light' of the lilies which are placed to encircle the Mother and Child, creating the atmosphere of peace and reverence of the Holy Night. Grey artichoke and onopordon leaves complete the arrangement.

109 The Nativity Mary Lee, *Whetstone, London.*

The magic of the nativity is portrayed by the subtle colouring and the clever arrangement of this composition. The cream figures merge into the cave which is made from driftwood. The glittered frame to the cave consists of gourds, walnuts, and flowers made from honesty and pine cones; the straw-cloth drape makes a suitable background.

110　Purity Margaret Couper, *Cupar, Fife*

This gold and white arrangement is made with dried and artificial materials and is suitable for use in a centrally heated room.

The outline is of white plastic fern with preserved gilded aspidistra and ivy leaves. The flowers, which are the central interest, are made from gold ribbon. The gilded figurine adds meaning to the composition. *Photo: John G. Inglis, Cupar.*

111　Pickwickian Christmas Blanche Bedford, *Luton, Beds.*

Ivy, holly, yew and laurel make this Pickwickian Christmas arrangement with the apples giving colour to the picture. The antique inkwell and spectacles give the feeling of the period.

112　Edwardian Elegance Jean Taylor, *Knutsford, Cheshire.*

This Edwardian candelabra holds an arrangement of red roses, carnations, leaves of ivy and *Begonia heracleifolia*. It is an elegant arrangement for a traditional room at Christmas.

113　The Sparkle of Christmas *Members of the London and Overseas Association.*

This fascinating group of arrangements was the centrepiece at a London and Overseas Area Christmas Show.

114　Christmas Gift Jean Taylor, *Knutsford, Cheshire.*

The figurine carries aloft a gift of red

carnations and roses which would be so acceptable at Christmas, *Photo: D. Rendell.*

115　For a London Flat Mary Lee, *Whetstone, London.*

Driftwood is combined with plants and flowers to produce this charming arrangement. The plants are *Echeveria* and *Begonia rex* and the cut flowers are lilies.

116　For the Drawing Room Edith Wise, *Chelsea, London.*

This dainty arrangement on a candlestick has a small fern and ivy growing in John Innes No. 1 compost. The lachenalias and freesias are in a block of Oasis.

117　Pot-et-Fleur Violet Stevenson, *London.*

The container of this lovely arrangement is a composite one: the brass base of an oil lamp supports a bowl for holding the plants and flowers. The tulips are held in position on a pinholder and the daffodils are in a metal cone. Yellow crotons are placed at the top and the left-hand side, cryptanthus in the centre, and *Hedera canariensis* rests on the driftwood.

118　For the Town House Edith Wise, *Chelsea, London.*

This charming arrangement in a silver entrée dish is composed of a small fern, peperomia, bromeliad and tradescantia, all growing in John Innes No. 1 soil. The roses and freesias are in a small container hidden from view, and give colour to the arrangement.

119　Blue and Gold Marian Aaronson, *Upper Wanborough, Wiltshire.*

The dramatic colours of the strelitzia

flowers are repeated on the blue and gold wire which has been looped into a rhythmical pattern. The monstera leaves add further depth and another texture.

120 Kenyan Treasures Marian Aaronson, *Upper Wanborough, Wiltshire.*

Two stem husks of the monstera plant make a strong outline for the two scarlet anthuriums. The twirls of gum tree bark add further rhythm to the arrangement.

121 Thorn Construction Marian Aaronson, *Upper Wanborough, Wiltshire.*

Twigs of blackthorn have been painted black and arranged to make an abstract design. The vivid red rose adds the extra dimension of colour.

122 Metallic Splendour Marian Aaronson, *Upper Wanborough, Wiltshire.*

The cold sparkling quality of the stainless steel is contrasted with the warm orange-red of the kniphofia flowers. Two **monstera deliciosa** leaves complete the design.

123 Play on a Circle Jean Taylor, *Knutsford, Cheshire.*

Two gerbera daisies and black canes, which have been formed into circles, make this non-objective abstract arrangement. *Photo: D. Rendell.*

7 . FLOWER ARRANGING IN MANY COUNTRIES

GREAT BRITAIN

Phyllis Page

Flower arranging today has become an art practised in all parts of Great Britain and gradually during the past years it has changed from a drawing-room activity to an international art.

The governing body is the National Association of Flower Arrangement Societies of Great Britain, known as NAFAS. It is affiliated with the Royal Horticultural Society and has welcomed the affiliation of similar organizations all over the world.

Various sub-committees have been appointed to deal with the many facets of the movement, the main business being conducted by the council which is composed of the officers and representatives from each area.

One of the main aims of NAFAS is to raise the standard of work by instructing and training judges, demonstrators and lecturers. Tests are held, the standard of work is very high and it is the aim of all judges, demonstrators and lecturers to be placed on the national list. It fosters the love of flowers and encourages members to decorate their homes with flowers, however simply. It stimulates the interest in the growing of special plants for decorative use, as even small gardens can be stocked with flowers and foliage essential to the flower arranger. It aims to give pleasure to the sick and elderly by the regular arrangement of flowers in hospitals and many worthy causes and charities have benefited as the result of shows and exhibitions. These are sometimes held in stately homes where the public has the opportunity of seeing the priceless heirlooms enhanced with the beauty of flowers. Large sums of money are raised for the restoration of historic churches and cathedrals through exhibitions.

The National Festival is the highlight of the year. This is held in London and the provinces alternately.

There is a great interest in the Japanese style of flower arranging and under the auspices of Ikebana International this art is taught and exhibitions are held.

It is, however, the western style that appeals to most people in Britain. The garden and the countryside offer such a wealth of flowers and foliage that it is within the means of most people to have flowers in their home.

The country is divided into twenty areas on a geographical basis. The areas are the intermediate step from national to club level and deal with much of the administrative work. Shows are organized once or twice a year and clubs within an area combine to stage exhibitions. Courses for judges, demonstrators and lecturers are held and successful candidates are added to the area list.

There are, to date, well over 950 clubs throughout the country. Some are purely Flower Arrangement Societies while others are sections of long-established Horticultural Societies. Women's Institutes and Townswomen's Guilds show considerable interest in the art. The number of members in a club varies from district to district, some of the larger ones having several hundred members. Meetings are usually held once or twice a month for a demonstration, lecture, show or exhibition and classes are run for beginners and less experienced members, where individual instruction is given. In many districts the local education authorities organize series of evening classes.

A teachers' association, with over 500 members, has

been formed which works in conjunction with education authorities and the City and Guilds of London Institute.

The Headquarters of the National Association of Flower Arrangement Societies of Great Britain is: 21*a* Denbigh Street, London, S.W.1. *The Flower Arranger*, a quarterly magazine full of information and interest, is published and many other publications that are helpful to club secretaries, organizers and flower arrangers generally.

AUSTRALIA

Estelle Normand

Flower arrangement in Australia has never been as popular as it is today and during the last five years the added interest of Ikebana has spread across the continent. The need for good and unusual materials has stimulated gardening to such an extent that effort is made to provide flowers and foliage all the year round.

Australians have become very conscious of their native flora and use it to a great extent in their flower arrangements. Each state has its own wealth of native flowers but many of these are protected and are not available to pick at will. Western Australia, divided from the rest of the continent by desert land, has a wealth of flowers found nowhere else in Australia. From August to December the Bush is colourful with hundreds of different wild flowers and station owners allow some enterprising enthusiasts to pick the flowers and send them by air to the eastern states. Blackboys (*Xanthorrhoea australis*) with spear-like leaves two to three feet long and a flower spike five to ten feet high, resembling a great bulrush, together with the smaller, more compact blackgins are examples of the interesting plants typical of the country.

Flower arrangers comb the ocean beaches for driftwood, sometimes in the form of roots of trees uncovered by the high tides, but the best place yet known for beautiful shapes and colour is on the sand dunes of the south-east coast of South Australia.

159

Dried arrangements have become popular in the homes. Flowers are expensive, the climate hot, gardens are smaller and there is less leisure time in this modern world, so a background of dried material is used with a changing centre of interest of flowers in season. I have maintained large arrangements in urns during the last six years in the National Gallery of Victoria, using a great variety of dried materials.

There is a great demand for demonstrators in floral art and most women's clubs like to include some demonstrations in their schedules. Mass arrangements in the Constance Spry style are still used at flower shows, in churches and galleries, but Japanese arrangements are very popular. Mr Norman Sparnon, a master of the Sogetsu School, Tokyo, resides in Sydney, New South Wales, and many have benefited from his teaching. Even those who have not studied the art have been influenced by his style. Ikebana arouses an awareness of nature and the search for unusual material is unending in such a vast and untamed country. A car drive of a hundred miles to rescue a native fern from the road-maker's bulldozer would be no rare occurrence.

Most of the towns have horticultural and floral art societies and usually hold a meeting each month. Speakers or demonstrators are invited and members exhibit in floral art and cut flower classes. The larger societies hold four shows a year, when an attendance of three thousand visitors in one day is not unusual.

The following photographs are of Australian arrangements:
4, 66, 67, 70, 71

NEW ZEALAND

Barbara Cave and Vera Tucker

Artistry and originality are evident in the flower arrangements done by New Zealand flower arrangers – never more enthusiastic than over the past few years. Visitors from overseas comment on the high standard of work that is done, whether in contemporary line or abstract design or the more traditional mass display. Each city in New Zealand from Auckland in the north to Invercargill in the south stages keenly competitive floral shows three, four or five times each year.

Since the formation of the Floral Art Society of New Zealand in 1965, floral art, which till then had flourished widely under the aegis of horticultural societies and garden clubs, has acquired some degree of unity of aims. This has been achieved with more than 88 clubs and over 3,700 members; though it is noticed that most members still work keenly for their original organizations.

With the concentration purely on floral art the emphasis on improving skills and learning the technique of judging and staging for flower shows means that even more progress is being made. The Society has arranged for tours of overseas demonstrators.

Classes are now given in all large centres of New Zealand by skilled arrangers. Many of the classes are run in conjunction with Polytechnic education, women's clubs, etc. Although there is an increasing tendency to flat living, particularly in urbanized areas, the majority of New Zealanders have gardens and grow their own flowers and shrubs. Even with the trend towards smaller sections, people here, both male and female, have always had a do-it-yourself attitude, and growing their own plants is one of the things they do very well. The result is that, though some prefer to purchase the ultra-perfect florists, blooms raised by specialist growers, there is plenty of material for the flower arranger to use.

Beautiful stones for use as bases are available in many areas, pink marble from Hanmer, green stones from the Homer Valley and stones with gleams of silver schist from the Haast district – most flower arrangers return from their vacations with some treasures – slabs of stone, attractive pebbles or driftwood. Most of this driftwood has been brought down from New Zealand's famous mountain forests to the lake shores and can be found in all sizes from minute intricate gems to enormous contorted branches suitable for very large grouped decorations.

Our native flora is interesting in form and subtle in colour. Among the more vivid are kowhai, with masses of golden flowers, scarlet manuka and the brilliantly red clianthus or kaka beak. The puriri has shiny crinkled leaves and red globular fruit, while the pora pora has yellow and green fruit. The North Island abounds with arum lilies growing wild and the South Island has the mountain daisies and mountain beeches.

The art of making arrangements which are large as well as those suitable for the average small home depends on the material available and New Zealand floral arrangers have a wealth of wonderful things from which they can choose when doing arrangements.

The following photographs are New Zealand arrangements:
38, 55, 74, 75

SOUTH AFRICA

Ida Ingle

The absorbing joy and satisfaction of floral arrangement has become part of a way of life in South Africa. In this country it is possible for the keen arranger to further the art by acquiring membership within such organizations as horticultural societies, floral art clubs, garden clubs, as well as those which are frequently convened under the auspices of the Women's Institute or the Women's Agricultural Association.

The benefits to be derived from membership may vary considerably, depending on factors such as efficient leadership or geographical situation. Since this is a land of vast space and great distance, it can be appreciated that opportunities of obtaining experienced lecturers and demonstrators are often limited.

In the absence of a central co-ordinating body, it would be difficult to assess the membership of the entire country; individual clubs vary considerably, from a few dozen to many hundreds. A desire for uniformity of standards resulted in the formation of a panel of judges functioning under different titles in each of the four Provinces of the Republic. That these may, in time, unite under one national name with one set of rules is an ideal which, as yet, has not been attained.

South Africans love to fill their gardens with the same annuals, biennials, perennials, shrubs or even fruit trees which may be found in other countries of the world. The varying climate renders it possible to cultivate much that is interesting from the desert bloom to the orchid which may be both rare and exotic.

The botanical wealth of the country is found in the sixteen thousand or more species of plants which may be said to belong naturally to South Africa. Horticultural shows of the Cape Province which feature this indigenous aspect are breathtaking in their beauty. The artistic flower arranger is thus adequately endowed with possibilities which may be limitless. Consider, for example, a single source – the Proteaceae family. It is a very large one consisting of several hundred species, specimens of which may be found in many parts of the country. Difficult as it is to narrow the field for comment, mention must be made of a few of these: the king protea (*Protea cynaroides*) with its silvery peak of flowers surrounded by large pink bracts often measuring twelve inches across – indeed, a worthy choice for the national flower; the evergreen silver tree (*Leucadendron argenteum*) which glistens on the slopes of Table Mountain at the Cape of Good Hope; the nodding pincushion (*Leucospermum mutans*) with its orange pin-head clusters, and the blushing bride (*Serruria florida*) – that pale pink gem with delicately flushed bracts which surround the bloom. Apart from the unusual beauty of this family, these hardy plants enhance their appeal by their excellent lasting and drying possibilities.

Remembering the history of the country, it is an interesting fact that many of the common names of plants in South Africa are based on the Dutch language, now translated into Afrikaans as well as English (e.g. suikerbos, sugarbush for protea).

The Cape Province provides a picturesque background between mountain and river for the lovely heaths which mass into wide expanses of almost solid colour. This family

of Ericaceae consists of over five hundred species indigenous to South Africa. The small bell-shaped or tubular
structure of the flowers provides the ideal choice for the
selection of filler or spiky material. Also growing at the
Cape are the long-lasting chincherinchees. The greenish-
white cluster of flowers opens into tapering formation to
last, as a cut flower, for six weeks – a fact which does not
seem to hold true of the yellow or orange species. Never-
theless, a great many have now been hybridized and
selected to become even more vigorous in order to improve
their export value to various parts of the world.

Of the great variety of indigenous plants which may also
have been hybridized, the following bulb or bulbous
flowers of interest to floral artists, are selected: arums with
their creamy-white spathes which grow happily in swampy
areas of land and stream under ideal conditions of growth;
the yellow, gold or pink species which differ from the white
in their preference for dryer soil; agapanthus (white or
blue), freesias, gladioli, nerines, tritonias, watsonias
(seventy species) and *Kniphofia* (tritomas) which are
known as red hot pokers or torch lilies.

Arrangers find much decorative interest, as well, in a
collection such as this: wild cotton (*Asclepias*) with their
large attractive lime-green balls, crane flower (*Strelitzia
reginae*), banana (for the handsome bracts which enclose
the flowers; the de-foliated stalks of sugar cane; seed-
heads of wheat, mealies (maize) and kaffircorn (*Sorghum*)
or even the flowers of trees such as the kaffirboom (*Ery-
thrina*).

Succulents should not be excluded for they are extremely adaptable plants, so much so that it would be
difficult to find places where they do not grow, even in
areas of high rainfall. Aloes are, without doubt, the most
showy of these soft-grey evergreens, adding the virtue of

much colour to winter arrangements. Many succulents such as mesembryanthemum or allied genera are unrivalled for dazzling colour in the garden, but are, unfortunately, of doubtful value to the art under discussion.

Sub-tropical conditions found in the Provinces of Natal and the Transvaal are favourable for the growth of many exotic plants which give artistic delight to the exhibitor. This is true of bixa, ginger, ixora, anthuriums, *Dracaenas*, crotons and many more.

This country offers great rewards for the adventurous arranger: sculptured, weathered woods from the Kalahari; driftwood on beaches adjacent to such forests as Knysna; burls of stinkwood or olive for attractive bases; quartz and semi-precious stones from the goldfields of the Rand or shells from the Indian Ocean. All these and related materials certainly contribute to the excitement of acquiring natural accessories for the required placements. A warm climate such as this provides the ideal atmosphere so conducive to the preservation of plant materials – flowers and foliage alike. Hence, there is a growing interest in dried arrangements which may also be used in conjunction with the fresh.

Visitors to the flower shows in South Africa will readily observe the western adaptation of eastern concepts in the decorative exhibits, and will note the feeling for design in all its aspects. With instruction and opportunity, comes the desire to be artistically venturesome. Indeed, this is more of a challenge where the country is essentially arid; under such circumstances, the distinct preference for line and line-mass may be understood and appreciated. On the other hand, the abundance of materials often used in mass arrangements, undoubtedly reflects the profusion of plant life so readily available – a factor inconducive to restraint. A further observation is the extent to which the shows may reveal susceptibility to certain influences, notably that of colour. Expression may tend to be consistently strong and vibrant, or subtle and subdued. Again, areas may adopt the highly stylized design, while others may show greater freedom of approach. All is but a means to an end which is distinctly personal and individualistic.

Ikebana is fast gaining favour. Indeed, many members have visited Japan in order to become better informed and have returned with new ideas and fresh enthusiasm.

The hunger for knowledge in the field of floral art may be said to be widespread, and leads to an intelligent evaluation of this most fascinating subject.

The following photographs are of South African arrangements:
44, 45, 95–98, 107

THE UNITED STATES OF AMERICA

Helen S. Hull

There is a difference between the garden clubs in America and the flower arrangement societies of Great Britain. Whereas in Britain societies are devoted to flower arrangement only, in America the study of flower arrangement under the National Council of State Garden Clubs is combined with the study of all aspects of flower show production: flower show practices, exhibiting, staging, judging and horticultural knowledge. Indeed, flower arrangement may be a minor interest and the study of gardening, landscape design, horticulture, community beautifying or gardening therapy may be of predominant interest. Our flower shows reflect these interests and by National Council standards must include as many classes for exhibiting horticultural specimens grown by the exhibitor as classes in flower arrangement. At the shows there are also educational exhibits, conservation exhibits and exhibits of community projects in which the clubs are engaged; and increasingly there are sections devoted to exhibits in classes designed especially for juniors.

Usually the flower show is held in a central place in the community and is open to the public who are normally admitted without charge, but sometimes a charge is made to raise money for some community project. Lately, because of the high hiring charges, clubs have been turning more and more to home and garden tours. In these, several houses and gardens are on display with flower arrangements in competition in various rooms of the houses. Horticultural sections are usually displayed in one of the houses and education sections in others.

Flower-show schools are held under National Council standards under the auspices of the member state federations. In order to be a certificated amateur judge, it is necessary to pass five of these three-day courses, each with a three hour written examination, attended over a period of three years. The applicant must also have won five blue ribbons in flower shows of National Council standard and must have served as a student judge during this period and have passed a 'reading examination' of background material consisting of twenty-five or more books. The National Council certificate as a judge of amateur flower shows if won must be renewed every three years by taking and successfully passing the written examination of a refresher course. Advanced courses are also given under the term, 'Flower Show Symposium'. Advanced certificates may be had, one of 'Master' and 'Life' judge.

It is not necessary to have this cerificate in order to exhibit in a flower show, but those who go through the extensive course of study are the most knowledgeable and increase the standard of excellence. At least one of the courses is held in every state every year.

The instructors for the flower show schools are certificated by the National Council, although the horticultural subjects may be taught by specialists from the State University and principles of design or 'colour' may be taught by artists from special schools; but flower arrangement is taught only by National Council instructors who have mastered the National Council requirements of arranging and judging according to the point score system taught in all National Council flower show schools.

The interest in flower arrangement is universal throughout the United States among members of the National Council of State Garden Clubs and it is difficult to say whether there is a great difference in style from state to state. It is my personal opinion, however, that much originality and vitality in this subject is now coming from the West and Midwest.

Although Japanese flower arranging is not taught in any of the schools under the National Council, many flower arrangers have fallen under the spell of modern Japanese and are using plant material as shapes and forms with little regard to its character or beauty as a plant. One often sees artificial material being used, not only grapes and other fruit but also artificial ferns and foliage. This is not permitted in flower shows held under National Council standards but it is regrettably abroad in the country just the same. This, it seems to me, is a passing phase in an effort to explore new forms and to be 'original'. Nothing yet, however, has been devised to supplant the texture and colour of flowers lovingly arranged.

The following photographs are of arrangements from the U.S.A.:
46, 47, 68